MW01483930

Her notes, (some of) her words, her untold story

An authorized biography by Donnie

This book is dedicated to Gracie.

You started, and I finished it. I hope you approve.

always, d

Also by Donnie

Books:

Crumbs of Love (autobiography) published by I Universe
Agapi Mou (my beloved) published by Create Space

Plays:
After The Rain
'...tell momma, good-bye..'
Don't know the Colour of Rainbows, Actually
Dishin' With Divine
Milk the Cow

Musicals:
Tonya and Nancy: The Rock Opera (co-adapter)
Night with Day [Billie Holiday]
Soph: An Evening with Sophie Tucker (co-adapter)
'69- the sexual revolution musical (book, co-lyricist)
Gracie (book, co-lyricist)
Ari-Maria –[Aristotle Onassis/Jackie Kennedy] (book, co-lyricist)
J.C. 'a gospel according to an Angel' (book, co-lyricist)

Forthcoming:

Crumbs from the Table of Love (sequel to Crumbs of Love)
How do you say murder in Greece?
Spiti Mou
Lost History of Oregon: The Hoyt Hotel
Gracie Hansen's Paradise (pictorial diary from Morton to Seattle)

GRACIE

Copyright ©2011 by Donald I Horn (Donnie)

This is a work of non-fiction; Names, characters, places and incidents have been taken from newspaper articles, on-air interviews and with various persons, magazine articles, photos, letters and memos.

It should also be noted that when using a person's items they may misspell, use the wrong math, many things may be what the reader <u>thinks</u> should be corrected. As the author, I did that on some items, but other things were left as they originally were – I have always said, 'don't get mad at the messenger!'

"I was fat and 40 and I came out of the hills and I made it. My message is this: if I could, who the hell can't?"

Gracie Hansen

I'm dying.

Looking around at these walls just isn't the backstage that I thought I would be seeing on my last production. When they take one leg off and start on the other tomorrow, you know it ain't looking too good. My doc was just here. I trust him, but again, he's not the kind of guy not to trust.

If this is it, I just wish I'd been able to write and direct it in the way that I would have wanted it to happen. But, you don't get to do that on your final curtain call, do you?

I've been in and out of the hospital a lot over the past few years, and you know what? I think being out is so much better. There's a couple things I've made note of: the nurses for the most part are pretty good, and the food is pretty awful. I've never been in prison, but I think this must be how it feels; small rooms, bad meals, and so many do's and don'ts, I think the only difference is that after all is said and done, they send you a big fat bill.

I've started jotting things down in this little notebook that I picked up awhile ago. Did ya ever have one of these? It's a Livewire Steno Notes 80 sheet. They sure are convenient. Anyway, I said, "Gracie, it's about time you lay it all out for the world to read. I mean, if Miss Gypsy Rose Lee has the guts to bare it all, why not me? Of course I'm speaking of literarily baring it all! Because if you don't and you die, they'll think you made the whole thing up." So, that's when I started jotting down some thoughts with my favorite Flair felt tip marker in this steno pad, I've made it to page 4 and it starts...

Childhood (miserable)
Father's death- a lonesome fat little girl
Coxes
Louisiana (ride in rumble seat)
Columbia Apts.
Learning to cook
Babysitter suicide
Raspberry picking
Shows in garage
Smell of kerosene and mush
Gatuchios-grapes
eating cake in bakery
breadline movie

Morton
Leo elopement, disowned, miserable years
3-RH negative stillbirths
Sambo
worked in Reds Cafe
worked in bank
joined everything
PTA shows-6 years
Morton Methodists
Divorce-Pork?
Liquor store
apt in back (Compton's Mom Lily)
B.G.-Henry Pullen
Ross Dill-Agnes F
Esther-surgery-Mama

Fairhart's-learn to drive
Tom
canning-fruits
salmon, venison
cold-no heater

I'll try to finish the list later. There's a lot more to add. I'm told if you make a list first, you won't forget anything as you begin to write. Just watch, I'll still forget.

I'm tired. That damn nurse has given me some stuff for the pain. Thanks, Doll! Now I can't even see the paper.

Being born to a Sicilian father and a stubborn Louisiana mother pretty much tells you what kind of life you will be facing. My father, Sam Diana, I don't really know how he made it to Louisiana (as he was born in Sicily, Italy), but when he met my mother, Maria Mariable (she was christened Maria, but she always liked to be called Mary), he was smitten. How could you not?

I'll find some pictures and show them to you...they're in this box somewhere. I have to laugh, Dad was older than Mom, he was born in 1892 (at least that's what he had said to many who believed him), but I have just found out that he may have been born even 10 years earlier! Okay, so he didn't want to sound too old, right? But since Mom was born in 1904, even if he was born in 1892 that gives him twelve years lead...and then adding the other ten, that would make him twenty-two years older. I don't think it would have mattered to Mom, she loved him.

Everything about him, except for, as she would say, his flaw. He drank. He loved his liquor and wasn't too shy about letting anyone know it, too. During the prohibition, (which began in 1920 and ending in 1933) he found ways to get his drink and to hide it. He would hide his liquor in jugs under the floor in the closet. Wonder where my 'hiding' food came from?

I came along a little over a year after they were married, which was on June 3, 1921, and me? I came into this world screaming on August 21, 1922. At least I was told I was screaming, but doesn't almost every baby. Especially when they hit your fanny? And being born at this time of the year, I was a Leo; in fact a double Leo - my moon and sun signs were both Leo, giving me a double dose of trouble. As I have always said, 'that makes me twice as nice and twice as nasty.'

Dad was a barber, and a good one. Less than a year after I was born he headed to Vision City, Washington. He had heard that 'there were long-haired lumberjacks up there that need a good haircut and shave.' So, with very little convincing, he loaded up his barber tools, jumped on a train and headed to the Pacific Northwest.

It wasn't long until Dad settled in and got enough money for Mom and me to join him. What he was told was right; his business boomed and soon he started buying property, building homes and even opened a jewelry store. Within another year Mom found out that she was expecting another.

The town and life was changing. Vision City didn't sound much like a town people wanted to live in, so a new name was agreed upon, Longview. Longview is better? Long view from what? Anyway, about that time, my brother Carl was born in 1925. It is said that he was the first male child born in the newly incorporated city. He started out first in life at something. More than me.

Dad was smart, and he worked a lot. If he wasn't cutting hair, he was working on a house or selling jewelry. Even then I knew what it was like to appreciate things that glittered, sparkled and shined. And soon he had about three houses that he rented out. You would think that Dad being Sicilian and all, that he'd be Catholic. Well, he was, probably, but when Carl and I were small, he would drive Mom, Carl and me over to the First Christian Church on Sunday mornings and then come back when it was done. Mom, being Italian, was also born as a Catholic, but she left and became a charter member of the First Christian Church of Longview. She would say, "Sometimes I'd like to spit on them." I think she was saying this about the Catholics, and here is another time I wish I would have had her tell me what she meant. There are so many things you wished you would have asked, but can't now.

What I hated about the old Italian women was, when they walked in front of a church, they would cross themselves. And if there ever was a time when I was with them, they made me do it too. *The Father, The Son, The Holy Spirit, Amen.* They would say it was a sign of respect, I thought, 'respect isn't something you shove down people's throats, you earn it.' I never told anyone that they had to go to church or believe in God. Don't shove religion down people's throats, it's an individual decision – one I chose not to follow. Besides, religion doesn't have to be grim. After all, God is the greatest humorist of all. Just take a look at some of the people he's created.

I will tell you, Dad and Mom were good to the two of us. They didn't seem to get into fights or anything; (except for his drinking) we had a good life. But that all came to an end. Oh, I remember this as if it were this morning. I was about seven, almost eight, and Mom asked me to go in and 'wake up your father.' So, I tried and tried. I gave up and went back to the table to finish my breakfast.

Mom asked "where's Daddy?" And I told her that I couldn't wake him up. She left the room, and the next thing I knew, I heard her crying. She wouldn't stop.

Dad died of acute indigestion at the age of thirty eight or forty eight, depending – some say 'he died of the drink.' All I can say, if he did, he died happy. May 18th will always be a very dark day for me. I loved my Dad, you only get one father, no matter what.

It is said, and I have been told so, that Dad was so well-loved and had such enormous popularity that when he died, the whole town closed for two hours of mourning.

That's when life, our lives, changed forever. Mom wasn't the same for quite awhile; poor Carl was five and kept looking for his Dad. You see, Dad would put Carl on one shoulder and a jug on the other and parade around. I missed Dad too, I still do. He always smiled and made the world seem easier. Mom's Dad, my grandfather, came all the way up by train from Shreveport to help take Dad's body back for burial. Just as we were about to leave, both of us kids got chickenpox and we then had to wait an additional couple weeks. I think about that now and wonder, 'they held a body for over three weeks? How did they make it from not stinking.' Again, something I should have asked, but never have – or probably never will.

I don't remember much of the train ride, just that it seemed like it took forever. Once we reached Shreveport, Mom, Grandpa and the others went away, probably to finally bury Dad. Carl and I were left in care of this older colored man which, in turn, left us in this large room with food – lots of cakes, cookies, breads, and the smell. My heart rose to my tongue – I had made it to heaven and I didn't have to die. Grandpa was a baker by trade and he owned his own bakery. I knew then I was born into the right family. In my reach were things I could only have dreamt of. Yes, Mom baked, but in this very room were smells and sights I had never imagined. As Carl played with his toys on the ground, I walked past each glass case as if it were filled with jewels. I kept thinking, 'how could Dad have been a barber smelling dirty hair all day long, when he could have had all this?' Mom sat me down one evening and said that we had to stay. "I'm going to have to do something, so I'm going back to school, just like you." Even at eight, I knew this was wrong. First my Dad not wanting to be a baker and now my Mom going back to school, I truly was born in the wrong home. Of course, except for the bakery downstairs. But, true to her word, off she went. She would pack my lunch alongside hers and leaving Carl with Grandma Lena, off to school we'd go. Me, to grade school and

Mom to cosmetology school. In what seemed like no time, she graduated. I mean, it's only been around six months since Dad died and here she is graduated, and with two certificates! One from the Ernest Baum Products Company completing satisfactorily a course of study prescribed in 'Artistic' Croquignole Permanent Waving on November 10th, 1930, and from the Louisiana State Board of Cosmetic Therapy on November 20th, 1930. I guess baking wasn't in her blood, but why was she following after Dad? I have to chuckle now, I think shouldn't the certificate say weaving instead of waving? Maybe that's where I got my flair for raising my hand in a stance? I really don't think they gave 'artistic' awards for waving, if so I would have made sure I got one!

Oh, one day while Grandpa was away, Carl was sleeping, I went down to the bakery, snuck behind the counter and pulled out a large chocolate cake. The smell was intoxicating and the taste! The taste was overwhelming. The next thing I knew the platter with some crumbs were in my lap – I had inhaled the whole thing! The old colored man who worked for grandpa was looking down at me, "missy, what have you done?" With frosting all over my face, I looked up and just smiled. Whatever was going to happen, it didn't matter. I had struck gold. If this was heaven, take me now! But it wasn't, and I was never permitted to be in the bakery alone again, even as the years passed – which is really a good thing. One bite of anything isn't enough, especially when something tastes that good.

After Mom's graduation, she immediately got a job. So our lives settled into a pattern; Mom worked, Grandpa worked, Grandma Lena watched after Carl as he grew, and I went off to school.

Living in Shreveport was much different than Longview. Its population was around 76,000, which is much larger than any city I was used to. Having been born there, Mom knew her way around and she seemed to enjoy each day, except for one thing - the rain. 'It rains here more than it does up north, but thank god it doesn't get cold.' That is one thing I even to this day believe, give me sunshine any day, I cannot stand rain, snow or cold. Why does man have to be so miserable when there's warmer places to be?

And that's what living in Shreveport was, it was warm, comfortable and actually great. But, like everything in life, just when you see a straight road and things going smoothly, there's a bump. This one, though wasn't just a bump.

You see, for quite awhile Grandma Lena wasn't herself. She was holed up in her bedroom and wouldn't see us very often. Grandpa would work less time in the bakery, oh, he'd be down there around 4 am and close up at night, but he would, during the day, make more and more trips up the stairs and into their bedroom.

Grandma Lena had a laugh that could fill a room, but now? Stillness. I'd try to do my homework, but I'd find myself more and more tapping my pencil against the pages instead of using it to write.

Mom had a ritual to where she would kiss Grandma Lena as the last thing she did when she was leaving for work in the morning and the first thing she did when she came home at night.

One day I came home to find the bedroom door open so, without thinking I walked right in and the bed was empty. I threw down my books and ran down the stairs where I found Mom behind the counter. "Mom?! What are you doing here and where is Grandpa and Grandma?"

Mom looked over, reaching for my hand, then leading me around the case filled with those delights that I couldn't resist, finally sitting me down by the front window. "Grandma Lena is very ill." She tried with all her might to keep herself composed, but I could see, even with my young eyes, that 'very ill' was more than 'very ill'. "Grandpa has taken her to the hospital to see what is wrong."
"She will be all right, won't she?"
She pulled me into her chest, "That, I do not know."
I could smell her skin. It smelled of roses. When she finished in the bathroom, either bathing or getting ready to go to work or bed, I would try to sneak in just to smell the roses. When I close my eyes now that's what I think of when I remember my Mom.

It wasn't too much later that Grandma Lena died. She died of diabetic complications. At that time, I didn't know what that meant, but now? Well doll, that's why I lay in this bed today. They say it's hereditary, and seeing Grandma Lena go through it, my Mom and now me, I think this one the docs got right.

Grandma Lena's death was different than Dad's. I don't know if it was because I was older, but what I remember clearly was Mom coming over to the couch, sitting down and crying. All I could do is reach over, touching her shoulder, I said, "The angels needed her to help out with Dad. He's a handful up in heaven – probably still looking for his jug."

And then she started to laugh. Tears rolled down her cheeks. She turned and hugged me. "You just might be right."

This was the first funeral I was allowed to attend. I didn't understand much, but what I did understand was it wasn't a happy affair. I vowed right then that I would learn about this thing called death and dying, and even to this day I'm working on it. It's one of those things that you can't put off. I would ask Mom about it and she would say, "They've learned the secret." I didn't like that answer, because I would try very hard not to ask what every child would ask, "So, what's the secret?" I did that once, and Mom said, "You'll find out, but hopefully not for a very long time."

After the funeral, Grandpa started to wear black. He seemed to stay downstairs more and Mom worked less away from home and more time down in the bakery. She also seemed to play more with Carl or helping me with my school work. I needed the help. God bless Mom and her patience, because school work was not my strong suit and well, as I moved up in grades, and the class work not getting any easier, I struggled more and more. You have to admit, it was hard to sit in the apartment over the bakery and not want to run down and grab a twist, piece of cake or a slice of bread, maybe that's why even today I struggle with my weight, or it's just the Italian in me. Food is one of our best friends.

But, also, I just wasn't a good student. I didn't care. Wasn't there more to life than school? I said that then, but now, I wished I would have studied harder. I could have used some of that knowledge along the way.

I guess you could say, mother not like daughter or vice versa. Here I was struggling at school and Mom was excelling; in short order she got her two certificates and now, a driver's license. Grandpa did not quite understand, and he made it very clear how he felt about her getting the driver's license. What I guess was the 'one step over the line' was when she went out and bought a brand new 1934 two door Chevy with a rumble seat! When she drove that up to the front of the store and got out – I heard him all the way upstairs. He argued, stating that she didn't need such a contraption. Mom, with her beauty, wit and charm, smiled and said, "I needed it, because." No further words were ever spoken between them about the car. How come that has never worked for me?

The car wasn't used much as Grandpa still felt it impractical, and Mom obliged him. That said, when Sundays rolled around and Mom would get us kids together to drive out to the park or through the countryside, Grandpa didn't object to tag along, "just to make sure everything went all right."

It was a good thing she did get her license and the new car, because early 1935, I'm trying to remember exactly when, but one day Mom walked into the room while I was doing my homework (yah, I know, it seems like that was all I was doing, but believe you me, I spent a long time doing it because, as I've said before, I was not good at school) and she sat down at the table with a letter in her hand. "You know we're in a depression, don't you?" Since everyone talked about the word a lot I just nodded my head. Sure, I thought. Who wouldn't be depressed? Dad gone, Grandma Lena gone, the bakery didn't have a lot of customers – me not being able to enjoy the goodies down there - not a lot of things to be happy about. She continued, "we need to head back north, I'm going to tell Grandpa, so don't be surprised if there's some raised voices." Now, being twelve years old, you knew what that meant. I picked up my pencil and pretended to go back to my homework as Mom headed down the stairs to the bakery. Luckily, Carl was playing with some friends because the words weren't just raised, they were loud! To me, it was like when you boil water and it gets so hot it starts spilling over the sides and hitting everything in sight; well, let me tell you, Italians know how to speak their minds. And that water wasn't just spilling over the sides it was spewing over like a volcano.

After awhile, Grandpa appeared at the top of the stairs and nodded at me, "my little one, I will miss you." I jumped up and hugged him with all my might. I didn't know why, but I knew that this man, who was tall and strong and had been my rock for these past several years, wasn't going to take the journey with us and I was not happy about that. I can still feel his strong arms around me, those are hugs you never forget. He never said goodbye, how could any of us?

Two days later, with the car filled, taking turns crying, hugging and waving, Mom drove away, down the Dixie Overland Highway, or as some know it as US Highway 80, toward Dallas then up to Washington State.

Now that I look back on it, no wonder Grandpa argued with Mom. It was plain crazy for a woman of thirty-one years of age with a near thirteen-year-old girl and an eight-year-old boy to drive halfway across the country.

The car was crammed with our clothes, some books and a lot of hope. Mom allowed Carl and me to ride in the rumble seat – but going backwards over narrow roads and high cliffs without guardrails made Carl very scared. I ask myself now, why would change you let anyone ride in a back of a car, riding backwards, anyway? Isn't that the trunk! Thank goodness the car wasn't that old, but still, really, what was she thinking? She was a woman on a mission – no stopping her.
I tried to get her to let me drive, "I'm almost old enough." Carl would snicker and Mom would keep her eyes on the road, "That's it darling, you're just almost."

After many days and too few stops which Carl and I would have liked, we crossed the Columbia River and finally pulled into Longview.

Mom didn't waste any time when we hit town. Maybe it was the long drive or tired of being on the road, or having two young children in the car for that long of a time, but she headed right over to the West Coast Savings and Loan. Parking the car, she said, "Look kids. There's some business I have to attend to. You two must behave yourselves. I know it's been a long journey and once I conclude everything, we'll get an apartment.

Grace, I'm depending on you, and Carl you don't disappointment me, all right?"

Within seconds, Carl and I were shown seats and Mom was escorted into the manager's office. What I got out of the raised voices was that the Savings and Loan held the mortgages on an apartment building and a couple houses Dad had built. And Mom's mission was to figure out how to get money from those properties.

Mom never raised her voice unless she needed to make a point, and what came out of the office was a voice louder than I had ever heard. "Look, I know times are tough, but we can't let people just live there without making their rents. I have bills to pay and children's mouths to feed."
The manager seemed to keep his cool, replied, "Well, Mrs. Diana, our district manager is here today from Centralia and I'm sure he'll be happy to discuss the matter with you."

Just about the time he said it, up walked a very tall, very handsome man with a beard. She looked over and said, "I'm sorry, this is your 'District Manager?'"

He chuckled, and reached out his hand, "Ma'am, I'm George Barner, excuse the beard, it's for Centralia's Pioneer Days festivities."
She extended her hand as well, "I see."
He continued, "I know this may seem backwards to you, coming from Louisiana and all."
She straightened right up, "Actually, we lived here in '30, but being gone for five years, some things have changed." During

their conversation, George was filled in on her years away; the death of her husband, that she had two small children and the need for the income. Unbeknownst to her, he had become quite popular in Lewis County for helping people stay in their homes by allowing them to just make the interest payments on their homes. So after Mom explained her situation, George began telling her his ideas on 'making things right.' Well, I think Mom saw something in this man; as they talked, she melted and became very receptive to his ideas.

Why Mom didn't move us into one of Dad's apartment buildings, I guess that's another question I will never have answered, but she found us an apartment over a movie theatre. I was not going to ask, was I? I mean, not only over the Columbia Movie Theatre, it was also Empire Drugstore with a soda fountain and her own beauty shop. Once she got Carl and me situated into school, she started setting up her beauty shop next to the theater. I don't know if it's Daddy's old barbershop or not, it seems like it must have been, because it was really easy for her to get the ball rolling, right?

Now, I had never seen a movie until one night Mom, Carl and I went down into this wonderful lobby, then into this vast room with a large screen in front of us. The chairs were red plush velvet that rocked and there was this smell of popcorn in the air. Slowly the lights went down and then the sound from that large screen filled my ears. I had found the purest joy that I had ever known; it was right there on the screen, magic happened. The screen was filled with costumes, loads of jewelry, intoxicating music and those dance numbers. I was hooked. All of that glitz on one stage. When the light would come up I wanted to scream, "just two more minutes!" I would wait until most of the people left the theatre and I would sit, thinking about what I saw. Cakes are one thing, but movies, they are the icing I had been looking for.

Well, I have to tell you something. Remember I said I wasn't good at school work and that I had 'distractions'? Well, I'm in trouble again. First it was the bakery with the wonderful smells and the memory of the chocolate cake! But, now a movie theatre? Talk about a real motivator. My homework was done so fast once I found out that we could get into movies for free.

I knew that I had to at least get 'good grades', because if they dropped even a bit, the owner would be told that I wouldn't be allowed to watch the movies.

Each week a new movie would play and sometimes a double feature. How could you not go down and watch? The ones I remember were *Top Hat* with Ginger Rogers and Fred Astaire and *Curly Top* with Shirley Temple and one of my all time favorites, *The Gold Diggers of 1935*, a Busby Berkeley musical starring Dick Powell and Gloria Stuart.

Okay, my first love is food, but right next to that, was and still is - movies. I had found something that wouldn't put any weight on me, and actually helped me get my homework done. It didn't matter that I was a bit overweight and short, no, what mattered was that I was shown something that I wanted to do when I grew up.

Luckily, there would be another showing tomorrow or later that afternoon if it was on Saturday or Sunday, and there you would find me coming in being absorbed with movie magic. Carl too liked the movies, but only the westerns and adventures like *Mutiny on the Bounty* or *Tumbling Tumbleweeds*. Just like a boy. Right?

With Mom working again, and with George's help, money wasn't an issue as it once had been and soon we moved into a house, I think it was one Dad owned. And, then, not too long after, George began to come over to court Mom.

It felt awkward having a man sit at our table. I mean, it had been almost a year since we lived with Grandpa, and this definitely was not Grandpa! Being almost thirteen, I knew what was happening, but Carl thought it was just great having a guy around.
One day I asked Mom, "So where is this leading to?"
She smiled, "Leading to not having to worry." That was that. The next thing I knew, Mom and George were married, what a great Christmas present, right? It happened in 1936 because I remember we had to leave Longview and move to Centralia.

Leave again, a place that was home and move to a new city and one that had a surprise waiting for us all. Or for Carl and myself. Mom said that she married George then so he could go see the University of Washington Huskies play at the Rose Bowl, which they didn't that year, but they did go to Los Angeles while Carl and I were farmed out friends. Oh, they did attend the Rose Bowl, 'wasn't that part of the excitement of New Year's Day?

Being in Los Angeles, you had to go to the Rose Bowl.' God bless, she became a football widow even on her honeymoon.

Anyway, after winter break, we changed schools. And the very first day of school, a girl walked up to me and said, "So, you're George Barner's new daughter."
I said, "I guess."
"Well, don't think you can get away with a lot, just because he used to be the ex-mayor and all."
I was floored. My new stepfather not only was a bigwig in a Savings and Loan but also an ex-mayor? I think you could have knocked me over with a feather. What else about this man was there that we didn't know? Okay, at least he didn't go to prison for robbing a bank or anything, but shouldn't we have been told a little something? Well, come to find out, George had a past. Yep. He had been the youngest mayor of Centralia. Okay, not a big deal. Divorced, no children. Okay, again, no biggie. But, while in office, he led a crusade to subdue bootleggers. I found a photo of him from 1923 with members of the religious and temperance club leaders joining him on his campaign to clean up the city of illegal saloons. And, in 1925 a gun was pulled on him by a transient. Then, within half hour later, the transient shot and killed a Seattle attorney. This man wasn't just a stepfather, he had a past and I liked him more because of it.

George did take time with Carl and me, especially teach us some rhymes. These times were the ones I remember the most to be full of love for a man who became the father that I had lost. No, George couldn't take away Daddy, but what George did was give me a sense of the fact, it's okay to just be you. Here's a couple that I can still remember...

One day Silly Sally was swimming in the ocean,
And along came a huge ship
It ran right into Silly Sally
But Silly Sally just laughed and laughed
Because she was used to <u>hard ships!</u>

Okay, here's another...

One day Silly Sally was walking down an alley,
When a big, bad, scary man came down the alley
That big man tore all of Silly Sally's clothes off
But Silly Sally just laughed and laughed
Because she knew those clothes wouldn't fit
that BIG MAN!

On that one, I remember I would laugh and laugh. I would say, "poor Silly Sally, she needs some help."

Bored. I was bored. And doll, that is not a good thing. Especially being fourteen and bored, right? Here I am in high school, and wanting to do something. So, I majored in drama. Someday I was going to be on the silver screen, right up there with Ginger Rogers. Or, IF I was going to be up on the silver screen or on any stage, I would have to start somewhere. But, my luck wouldn't have it. I wasn't cast in any featured part. I've always been a frustrated ham, yet it finally came to me, 'you've always been the little fat girl...and you never get the romantic part being like that.' But what I did do was become the feature editor of the school newspaper. If I couldn't be in it, I would write about it.

Okay, here's something I wasn't going to share, but I might as well. At the new house, that's what Carl and I called it, the 'new house', there was a garage. So, with permission, I turned it into a little theatre. I invited all my 'new' friends from the neighborhood over and we started putting on skits. Boy, did we have fun. I would try to remember what I saw at the movies and then put some of it on stage. Carl wasn't too keen on joining in, but the rest of us had a blast. School was boring, but I was going to make the best of my life at home. To add some 'Hollywood' to it, we would charge a nickel for anyone to come see it. And, behold, they did!

Carl and I found our footing in the 'new house'. George was gone a lot, traveling around the state, but when he was home, it was family dinner no matter what. And Mom, for a while, stayed home to 'manage the house'. I guess she managed pretty well, because one afternoon she asked Carl and me to sit down with her at the table. Now, to me, every time this has happened, either someone died or we moved. I wasn't too sure, but I hadn't seen her cry so I didn't know what to expect. I mean, Mom was sitting in front of us with a smile on her face, her hands all fidgety. She finally spoke with a quiver in her voice, "Now, I know you two are older, Grace you'll be turning sixteen soon and Carl, my, thirteen. You two have grown up and…" She began to cry. We both sat there looking at her. But the tears she was shedding weren't tears of hurt, "I'm going to have a baby." And then her head fell into her hands. Did I hear that right? She was going to have a baby?

Carl's voice squeaked a bit, "A baby, here?"

Mom laughed, "Well, where else would we have it be?"

I sat back in my chair. A baby. Here I am about to go into my junior year of high school and my mother was going to have a baby?

Jeanette arrived in January, almost two years after Mom and George were married. So, you can't accuse her of 'having to get married'.

The house sounded and smelled different. It's not that I didn't want a baby in the house, but when you are almost sixteen, the last thing you want to do is hear your mother say, "Sorry honey, I can't help you, I need to change a diaper!"

Carl didn't seem to care one bit. Why should he? He was running home from school, then off doing his paper route. Then he would go and spend weekends, vacations and summers at various farms. He got to 'live' his love of cowboys. He'd come home and tell stories about his friends adventuring across the Columbia River in a rowboat (which if Mom knew she would have killed him or she would have died of worry) or learning to fire guns and go hunting. He was living a life of a boy in the wild west, as he would call it. He was growing up and being Carl. And me? Home, after school doing home work, helping Mom and trying to find excuses to get out of the house.

Somehow we all survived. Mom seemed happier than she had been in years, George was always trying to include Carl and me in everything. In fact, when the 1939 World's Fair in San Francisco was announced, George thought it would be a great family vacation. "It's called the Pageant of the Pacific, with a giant 80-foot statue of Pacifica, goddess of the Pacific Ocean." We were all excited. George helped us understand the massive scope of the Fair. "An island was created out of nothing for the Fair and it's also a celebration of two large bridges being completed, one being The Golden Gate." Even with a baby in tow, we made our way, like many, to the city by the bay. And it was wonderful. There was Gayway amusement section, many fountains, dancers and even the Sally Rand Nude Ranch! When I went over to look at the exhibit, Mom pulled me away. "Honey, that is not something you should be looking at." I laughed, "they are only women like us. Besides, I think I could have done better."

It was glorious, even with just a two lane highway from Centralia all the way to San Francisco, a trip that took two full days to drive.

That trip was the family trip. We as a family never took another one together. I was just entering my senior year, Carl was right behind and well, Jeanette was just beginning to walk.

I did not know it at the time, but what happened in 1939 would be part of my life in years to come. Sally Rand actually had been at the Chicago World's Fair in 1933, where in the depths of the depression her act was the about the only one that made money.

Once 1940 rolled around it was time for me to graduate. And, I'm proud to say that I did. Somewhere there is a high school diploma with my name on it from Centralia High School. I stood with a class numbering 165 on May 29th and walked across that stage and received my diploma. When I opened it up, it was blank. What? Hadn't I made it to the finish line? Then someone must have heard me gasp and they began to chuckle next to me and whispered, "You get the piece of paper after the ceremony. They give everyone blank folders so that way, they can't screw up." What a relief. I, to this day feel that the school administration thought, "graduate her or else, she'll hold everyone else back."

With my certificate, I was now free. I was on my own. Or so I thought. You see, I had been saving money and courage to head to New York. I was going to live out my dream of being on a stage, one way or another. The whole summer I was drumming up enough courage to talk to my Mom. I know Mom and George had other plans, but I was determined not to go to college. It was my life and I was going to live it.

So, making sure that Mom had put Jeanette to bed, I walked into the kitchen. There she was, the one I had to convince, washing dishes. I was going to learn bravery this day, and that if you want to live your dreams you have to fight for them. Standing behind the kitchen chair, holding my head up high, I point blank stated, "Mom, I'm going to do what I've always wanted to do, I am going to follow my dreams."

Mom looked over her shoulder, nodded her head and proceeded to wash the dishes. "I'm going to study acting. And the only place to really do that, is New York City."

You could have heard a pin drop. She slowly turned to me and said, "You can't go traipsing off to New York all by yourself." She must have known that her tone had grown loud, as she turned and smiled, "Let's get an education under your belt first, then we'll see what transpires. I think registering at Centralia Junior College will do the trick. You'll start in the fall. So, if you don't mind, could you grab a dish towel and help me out?"

Did I say no? Did I argue or put up any argument? Nope.

Well, you can see how this is going to end, can't you? Well, I hate to disappoint you, no, I didn't make it to New York, then. I went down to Centralia Junior College and registered for fall term. I stuck it out, surviving three months – one long quarter. I kept saying, "I can do this, for Mom, I can do this." But I couldn't. The days dragged on. And after cutting up frogs and worms and all sorts of things in Zoology class, I called it quits. The only thing that came out of college was a relationship with a man, Leo Hansen. This was really the first time that I didn't tell Mom what was happening in my life. I hadn't told her or actually anyone outside the people at college about Leo. Why? Maybe a bit of rebellion, but also I guess, I believed I was old enough to have a life outside Mom, George, Carl and now Jeanette. I had just turned nineteen, so I was more or less legal. And wanted to live my life. So, I quit. I quit college.

And with that, I made my first adult decision. Leo and I went down to city hall and got a marriage license. My proud day was January 15th, 1941. I leaned to kiss Leo and he whispered, "in ten days baby, in ten days." Yep. We had to wait ten days, a 'waiting period', before we could officially marry. So, secretly, I began to pack certain things and slowly take them out of the house. Not everything, but things, that if Mom looked, she wouldn't notice them gone. Boy that was hard, trying to play it cool and not let anything change my plans. And on the tenth day, Leo, his brother and girl friend and I were standing in front of the justice of the peace. No more than ten minutes later we were pronounced Man and Wife –at precisely 3:30 pm, January 25, 1941- I became Mrs. Leo Hansen. I was excited, scared and petrified. But I now was independent from my family.

I say we eloped. Okay, we didn't. But since we didn't get my parent's approval, I *feel* like we eloped.

The events in the world should have told me that things were not going to go well. As I was beginning my new life, Charles Lindbergh was testifying before the U.S. Congress. He recommends that the United States negotiate a neutrality pact with Adolf Hitler, and you know how that turned out. Yep, World War II...and the same thing happened when I went to tell Mom and George. It was late in the evening. Carl was upstairs doing his homework, Jeanette already in bed.

Leo, with his arms around me, said, "Mr. and Mrs. Barner, I, Grace, we have something to tell you."

Mom sat quietly with her hands in her lap. George stood up,

"Well, first young man, who are you?"

I stepped forward and flatly said, "Mom, Dad, this is Leo Hansen, he's my husband."

Mom stood up, and charged directly toward me, pushing me into the French doors between the living and dining room. She was screaming, "How dare you! How dare you!"

My arm hit the door I think and the next thing I knew there was a big gash in my left arm. She had shoved me so hard that I had fallen into one of the glass panes. That made me mad. "Look, I have always, ALWAYS done what you wanted of me, but I'm not doing it anymore. Leo and I are married and that's it."

George tried to pull Mom away, "Leo, what do you do, for a living, I mean?"

Clearly shaken, Leo responded, "A logger."

That's not what Mom wanted or needed to hear, "A LOGGER?" Turning to me she started shouting again, "What have you done? I've raised you to have your own mind in matters, but honey, we're Barners."

Without really thinking I said, "No, I'm a Hansen now."

Mom didn't miss a beat, "Wasn't going to college and being someone important to you? I mean no disrespect to Mr. Hansen here, but honey, now you are just a loggers' wife."

"Mom, I'm not a loggers' wife. I'm Gracie Hansen. I will probably always be Gracie Hansen, and you watch it, I'll make something of myself, and some day, you are going to say, 'That's my daughter and I'm proud of her.' You just watch."

Mom began shaking her head, "By moving to Morton? Gracie, honey, you'll never accomplish anything living in that town."

"Mom, you've taught me that you can accomplish anything anywhere."

Leo grabbed me, "We'd better leave."

Mom leaned into George and began to cry, "Where will you go?"

Leo cleared his throat, "Morton. I have to be at work tomorrow."

George just kept holding onto Mom.

"I don't know when I'll be back for my things." And then I walked out. I walked out into the cold, into a new life. I never said this out loud, but inside I kept saying, 'Gracie, this may be the stupidest thing you will ever do.'

Leo drove the long winding road, past small towns, rivers, into the mountains and into the town that would be my home. Gracie, what have you done?

MORTON
Let me tell you right now, "Morton is only two blocks long."

And for awhile, a long while - Mom and I did <u>not</u> talk. For one thing, I couldn't drive, so I walked everywhere and you just don't walk to Centralia. And also, we didn't have a phone, there weren't a lot of those in Morton. But what I did do was get pregnant. Fat isn't something I wanted. When you are already a little plus around the waist, pregnancy just adds more on. Your waist grows. Leo was happy, but me? I got depressed. What I didn't know was that my Mom, too, was pregnant. Life marches on even when you have left it. The folks built a home overlooking Centralia on Seminary Hill. The address - 105 N Barner Drive. Someday I'll live on a street with my name! And then George bought Mom a tan 1941 Chevy Coupe. He kept his 1936 4-door dark grey Chrysler. Mom called it "the lumber boat", as it was heavy and loud.

I wanted to tell Mom about me being pregnant. It was like she could be my sister now, sharing baby clothes, stories and then, as I was getting up to make Leo dinner, a sharp pain went through my abdomen. My legs buckled. I began to cry as I looked down and blood was dripping from between my legs... "No! NO! This can <u>not</u> be happening. God, don't punish me for leaving home and marrying Leo. NO!"
Leo ran over, grabbing my arms, pulled me into the bathroom and on to the side of the tub. "I've lost the baby. My baby. It's my fault. All my fault." Leo held me, I could feel his breathing. Was he thinking the same thing? Was this payment for me not being a good daughter? We sat there not saying a word. Right

then, I knew there must not be a God, as he wouldn't do this – right?

Slowly, Leo pulled away. He took a wash cloth, after running some warm water on it, began to clean my legs. He then proceeded to pull me up and I stumbled into the bedroom. My head was light and I felt like I was going to throw up. He laid me down and pulled the heavy patchwork quilt over me. I cried and cried. He just sat rubbing my back and shoulders. I was a failure as a daughter, a wife and now as a mother.

The next thing I knew, Leo was kissing my forehead. "Honey, I have to leave for work. I've called Esther to come over and check on you." I nodded and went back to sleep.

For what I guess was most of the day, I slipped in and out of sleep. Closing my eyes helped me close out the world. I was empty.

It took a couple days, and help from Leo and Esther, I got back to what some would call a normal state. I began to function is a better word. There was no reason to confide in Mom now, was there? She, what I had heard, was ecstatic to be pregnant and George couldn't have been prouder. Leo kept putting his arms around my waist and saying, "Grace, darling, if it was meant to be, it was meant to be. Look, when you are ready, we'll try again."

And with Leo gone in the woods, walking is what I did. It is a wonder I didn't lose weight or learn about exercise. Soon, the sun started shining more, the tulips started blooming and my spirits started to soar. The winter had turned to spring and then before I knew it, summer and of course the Loggers' Jubilee, but back then it was called something like the Hillbilly Days. Second week of August like clockwork, and this was going to be my first experience. Leo was in heaven. What had been started in 1937 or '38 to help the loggers relieve the stress of their business and to show the younger generation how it was done in the 'good old days' when axes were used, not these new chainsaws – it was the biggest event for the little town of Morton.

I have to laugh, because early on, there was a mock 'hillbilly' wedding held on Main Street and plywood axes were sold as souvenirs. Wow...big time, right?

But, for Morton, it was. Tree climbing, log rolling, music and food. The town swelled during this time. Leo, being a logger, participated heavily in it. He loved this part of his life in Morton. I loved him for it, but what I didn't love was his further love of the drink. He, like Dad, loved the jug. During this time he always thought that it was all right for him to have more than usual. It wasn't until the years added up that I began to speak out, but at this time I was the good wife and just lived through the angry, the mean, the very drunk man called my husband.

But, at the celebration I had a good time. The next week, just like clockwork came my birthday and this year I was turning nineteen.

Welcome to old age, Gracie. I say that now with a chuckle...but then, I did feel old. Hadn't I been through a lot in just eight months? Then there was a knock at the door.

"Grace, you got a call, come down to Red's Cafe."

There weren't a lot of phones in town and Red's was a well - known cafe which had what we all called the 'community phone'. And when you got a call, you didn't waste time – get down there, get the news and get off – someone else might be calling. So rushing in, I picked up the phone and I don't know why, but I answered it by saying, "Red's Café, this is Grace."

On the other end was a voice that sounded frantic, "Grace, its George. Your Mom has gone into labor, she's going to have the baby today or tomorrow, just wanted you to know."

Not much else was said, but when I hung up the phone I shook my head, "I'm going to have to share my birthday with their kid?"

This would be my first birthday not celebrated with Mom and Carl. I didn't think anyone had remembered, but when Leo got home, he surprised me with a small box and inside was one of the prettiest things I had seen, a brooch with different colored jewels, it was sparkling back at me. I had always been an admirer of Mom's good jewelry, and even though I knew that this one wasn't expensive, right then and there I said, "I like this stuff a lot." I have to admit, even though it didn't cost a lot, Leo found my heart that day. Diamonds, even the fake stuff, always make me feel so much better.

Fortunately for me, George was born the following day. I have mixed feelings about saying this. He is my brother, all right, half brother, but why did he have to be born so close to me? I wasn't mad at him, or Mom, but it just felt like whoever God is, he was playing another trick on me. Yep, he'll get all the adoration, the presents, because he's new. Here is old Grace- just plain old. Who will always be nineteen years older than George.

And then I started thinking, "Shouldn't we at last go and see them?" Easier said than done, with Leo working odd hours in the woods, so, instead I went to Fairhart's Department Store, bought a card and mailed it.

August turned into September and then into darkness. Since Morton sat on one of the roads to Mt. Saint Helens and Mt. Rainier, tourist who trekked up through our little town, all spring and summer, but boy, with the first hint of cold-Gone!

Thanksgiving came and went that year and things got worse- the bombing of Pearl Harbor. 1941, which started off with hope, was ending pretty badly. No one really cared about Christmas. And to make matters worse, I didn't even hear from the folks, not even a card. They were probably too busy with their new baby, Jeanette and all. *Doll, you did this to yourself. Get used to it.*

I found that I was home more and more alone. Alone in Morton is not what you would call a thrill. I have to confess something right now. I do not have a tidy house. If I can put things back where they came from, that, would be a miracle. So even being alone I didn't find myself 'tidying up the house'. What I found was, I was pregnant <u>again</u>. Not something I was expecting, but Leo didn't like to use protection so, if I was to be pregnant, it must be so. I had an underlying fear that something might happen, like the last time. But every day I woke up, lived and found that things seemed to be fine. Until. I know, it happened when I was heading out to buy groceries right at the front door. A shot hit so hard from the lower middle of my back that I fell against the front door and then slid down the wall. Tears flowed and I began to cry out loud. "No! Not again." I reached up under my dress, then out, I found blood all over my hands. "Why has this happened?" I crawled inside and to the bathroom. I slowly pulled myself up onto the toilet and rested my head on the sink. I felt weak, like I couldn't move.

I don't know how long I was there, but the next thing I knew, Leo was shaking me, "Grace, there's blood from the front door to here...what happened?"
The only word that I can remember crossed my lips was "I..." and then I passed out. Now, once is not good, but twice, there has to be something wrong. And I wished that we knew at that time, but there was one tiny problem. Okay, it was bigger than just tiny. We didn't have the money to go to the doctor, so I, laying in the bed with the quilt over my body, I weathered another miscarriage. I don't know how I did it, or what made me push forward, but I did it. This time, I didn't even tell Esther.

What I did discover was, in the middle of the winter, laying in bed with nothing to do or listen to, Morton was boring. BORING! When I mentioned that to Leo he said, "If you're not cold and you're not hungry, what are you bitching about?" Boy, he was a load of sympathy, right?

The only thing I had to look forward to when I woke up in the morning was waiting for Leo to get home from work at night. On the calendar I also was checking off the days until Carl was to graduate from high school. That's right, here's Gracie all grown up and her baby brother was just about to break out into the world.

It had only been two years since I graduated and where was I? Married, two dead babies and sitting around watching the world go around me.

Winter passed into spring, and by mid June Carl was to graduate, and I wasn't there to watch him walk across the stage. And besides, how could I face Mom, George, Jeanette, now three, and baby George Jr. or George, as he was beginning to be called. It has been almost two years and silence was the only message that was sent. And with Mom having a new baby, holding him in her arms, it would have been almost too much to bear, that was a baby that could have been mine.

I'm truly proud of Carl though. Right after his graduation, he went to University of Washington on a football scholarship. Unlike me, he was going to make something of himself. But after one semester, he joined the Navy Air Corps – the world was at war and Carl was to be part of it.

If being stuck in Morton, at least there was the Jubilee to look forward to. However, the city officials decided that you can't celebrate something like logging when the world was at war. It would have been nice to have something happen around here, but then, 'who would have come anyway?'

For the next five years my life was hell. So, I wandered in and out of reading books. I think I read over 10,000 books, anything and everything I could get my hands on. Then I started taking courses in writing and hypnotism. It was easier to draw the shades to hide the darkness that was outside the window. True, it was dark inside, but I knew I could make my world less painful.

Something else I studied was metaphysics; you know, it's when you stare at something long and hard enough, and with plenty of faith, it will move. Well, I gathered some friends over at Mable Fairhart's house, and there we were all sitting around to looking at, oh, I don't know what, I think it was a little side table across the room or something, and I told everyone, "Now, you have to look at that object with 'united' faith it will move." We sat there, and stared and squinted and tried our best, but it did not move.

Standing up, Mable said, "it knows where it wants to be and it's happy exactly where it's at. Cake, anyone?"

That didn't stop me from studying it like everything else – something was bound to move in my life.

To make life even more miserable, I had a two babies die during the first couple months of their conception – both were stillbirths. I have been asking myself if I should count them as babies. That debate has been raging for the longest time. Am I right? The first two, I never even told Leo.

Ironic thing is that I was barefoot and pregnant again, is what I told myself when I discovered for the third time I was pregnant. It was fortunate for me that Leo was working all hours and didn't care about anything to do with me – all he wanted to do was eat and sleep. I prayed that this one time some miracle would happen. My breasts got bigger as did my belly. I put on weight I hadn't put on before and I kept feeling more and more that this one was the one. Sam Hansen was born and died a still born due to a breech of delivery on February 4, 1943.

The only reason Leo knew was when I wasn't home he looked at Fairhart's and at Red's – then he went to the Wheeler Tavern. That's when Melverna told him that she thought I was taken to the hospital. I cried myself to sleep. Sam would have lived if the delivery canal wasn't the problem. I decided right then and there it was me.

I pushed Leo away more and more, and when I did that, the more he drank. He didn't want me to work, as 'a woman's place is at home.' So, I ate, was depressed and was so close to calling it quits and running back to Centralia. But, how could I do that? Would Mom open the door and say, 'welcome home, honey, would you mind helping me raise a child?' As I think about it, it sounds really stupid, but back then I just wanted to have my Mom love me. Actually, anybody to love me.

It would be almost three years before Leo and I even started to become a couple again. I made his breakfast when he got up, lunch for work, and dinner when he came home, which was just enough to eat, change clothes and go to the tavern. I'd go up to Fairhart's and hang around the store, or head over to the Mobil station and wait for Esther to come home from her day as being a school teacher. One day she looked at me and said, "Grace, you've got to change out of this or you are going to die."
I looked at her and thought, 'aren't I already dead?'

Then, for the first time in years, I started feeling young again. I started playing with my hair (as best as I could), started fixing up my dresses and Leo started noticing me again. It was like a sign had been turned on and it said, 'Open for business.' And then what I feared most was that I was, you guessed it, didn't I learn from before? I was pregnant for the fourth time.

I stayed in bed most of the time, I kept reading the self help books so that I had 'positive energy' at all times. I would rub my stomach and tell stories of dreams and wishes and tell the baby that I loved it so much that I knew it was going to be born full and strong and that finally Leo and Gracie would have a family and everything was going to work out like I had imagined that January day in 1941. When I went to the doctor he came back with great reports. I got so excited when this full-fledged human being started kicking and pushing and making some days miserable to live, but other days pure joy. I couldn't contain myself. Leo acted like this proud peacock of a man – strutting around not knowing what to do with himself.

And, on March 20th, 1946 little Michael Earl Hansen was born. Unbeknownst to me, Leo had gotten Mom, George, Jeanette and George over to be there with me. We'd made up a little bit earlier, it was mom that broke the ice, wanting me to baby sit Jeanette and George while they went on a trip. Lord, when they were gone, George fell down on the furnace grating and received some heavy blisters. I thought sure I'd catch hell, but not this time, I guess they knew George was like any other boy, easy to get into trouble. But, right then, having her there, all the pain of years past seemed to melt away. She reached out and held my hand, "I'm here for you." is all she said. And to be honest, that is what I wanted to hear. No one believed that this was truly happening. In fact, we all held our breath and a baby shower wasn't thrown until a couple days before I went into labor. And what a baby shower it was. All of our friends had gone out of their way to decorate the house as well as make a little room off the dining room as a nursery for the upcoming bundle. I would sit on the dining room chair and shake my head, this really is it, this is how it is suppose to feel.

But, now the contractions, I have heard that they can be brutal, but nothing, and I mean nothing prepares you for the jolts of pain that run through your body. And within hours, a baby was pushed out of my body, a scream was heard from his mouth and the doctor said, "Grace, we need to get him to an oxygen tent." And that was my first glimpse of my baby. *I only got a quick*

Leo walked over and said, "You did good."

I had, hadn't I? And I sighed and fell asleep.

Michael Earl Hansen was born on March 20, 1946.
Michael Earl Hansen died on March 22, 1946.

My body ached. My voice screamed. I couldn't contain myself. "BUT HE LIVED." "I SAW HIM, HE LIVED!"

I was told later that George's brother, Don, who was the Fire Chief in Centralia, rushed a resuscitator truck over to Morton. But, about half way, he received a radio call saying it was too late.

Within a few days, I was sent home. The doctor was worried, as I had slipped into a deep depression at the hospital, and quit talking. Hell, I had finally brought a child into the world, and it still dies?

Leo brought me home, and even driving up to the front door, I began to sob. I just didn't want to go in – what, face the nursery without a baby? But, as he helped me up the stairs, and into the dining room, I looked over and the room was bare. Esther, Mom and some friends had gone over earlier and cleaned the house. And, there they stood, welcoming me home. Immediately, I fell into Mom's arms and just stayed. Leo turned around and walked out. He had stopped talking to me. I believe he thought it was all my fault.

After several days, Mom, George, Jeanette and George headed back to Centralia and Esther back to the store. I was left alone hours on end with shades pulled, in silence.

When I did visit the doctor, I couldn't even ~~beat to~~ held back talk about what had happened to Michael, or the other three. But after being examined, I blurted out, "Am I a freak or something?"

The doctor, god bless this doctor, turned, held onto my hand and sat down. Looking deep into my eyes he said, "Grace, you are going to think me mad, but I truly think you should try one more time to conceive."

All I could do was laugh. He apparently had never tried to bring a baby into the world with his own body! Having it begin to grow changes your feelings, your cravings, your anticipation, and then it all being destroyed with your body aborting it? But, for once, I sat quiet.

"What you have is what is known as RH Factor."

"RH Factor?"

"Yes, that's when, for example, if you are Rh-negative blood type, you may develop antibodies to an Rh-positive baby. If a small amount of the baby's blood mixes with your blood, which often happens, your body may respond as if it were allergic to the baby. This means you have become sensitized and your antibodies can cross the placenta and attack your baby's blood. It can become severe enough to cause serious illness, brain damage, or even death in the fetus or newborn which is called a miscarriage or an induced abortion or menstrual extraction."

"All right, that means, I really can't have a baby?"

"Not necessarily. What we should look at is seeing if you can have a baby girl."

I began to laugh. I couldn't stop. Was this doctor a quack? "Look, how do I choose to get pregnant with a baby girl?"

He looked down into his hands, "You don't choose, god chooses, I know, but if you tried and did get pregnant with a baby girl, her chances of survival will be higher than that of boys."

"So, you are suggesting that I get pregnant again?"

"If you want to try again, yes."

"I'll take that in advisement." And I left. How crazy was that?

Now, not only was I depressed because of living in a small town with nothing to do, my husband was drinking more and more and leaving me at home alone, I was being asked to 'think' about having another try at getting pregnant for the fifth or sixth time? WHAT? Even having Leo on top of me made me sick, it was like his sperm knew just where to go and attach themselves. And, yes within a few weeks, even though I didn't want to, I was feeling nauseous and I instantly knew that I was 'in the family way' again. Shit.

I chose not to tell anyone. I wore big dresses, went hardly anywhere and when Leo advanced on me, I finally admitted that

I was pregnant again. His reply, "you are as easy as an old sow." Thank you, dear husband of mine, that's exactly how I am feeling at the moment, too. The nine months passed slowly, and as I went into labor I reached over to the doctor and said, "don't tell me if it's not a girl." At the last push, there was silence and then a baby crying. *it died.*

Leo wasn't even there. The room was still, and two hours later, *he* died. I was done. I was not going to try – no matter how hard I was forced. The five deaths in seven years was enough for me- no, it was enough for anybody. *ever again.*

To shudder some of the bleakness from the four walls, I started thinking there was something more to Morton than just cooking meals for Leo and waiting for sunshine.

That's it! Cook. I can do that. I loved doing that. Something I am very good at, thanks to Mom. I bet there's a need for someone to cook some good old home-cooked meals. I searched and searched and that led me to Red's Cafe. Thank goodness for Melverna Hathaway and her husband. They took me in and gave me something to do. It wasn't a full-time job, but it was 'out of the house for a while' and that was enough for me. Now, Leo was a patron at their Wheeler Tavern and me – where did I get my phone calls? So, without much persuasion, I was hired, not just for cooking but for doing everything; a little cooking, a lot of cleaning and even waiting on tables.

When it was slow, and after everything was done that I could do, I'd sit down on the bar stool, look out the window and sip on a Coca Cola. I think that was where I got addicted to that stuff. Now, I've heard and I don't know if it's true or not, but it has been said that Coca Cola had the basis of cocaine in it. Maybe that's why it's different from Pepsi...but no matter what, I was hooked. Fortunately, Red's was just up the street from where we lived. Ha, everything was so close to everything else that you really didn't need a car.

space

One afternoon in mid April 1947, the phone rang and answering it, I heard my mother's voice. The news? Through the tears and after passing the phone to George, I learned that Grandpa Mirable had died.
Once Mom composed herself she asked, "Gracie will you come with me?"
Without hesitation, I joined Mom on the train and traveled to Shreveport for his funeral.

Even after losing all those babies, hearing my mother shed her grief tore me in ways I can not even describe.

Maybe it was the memory of the train ride that was still on both of our minds – Daddy's body rode along with us. But now it was just Mom and me. She started to talk to me, and told me things that I had missed. "You see, after we left for Longview, Grandpa sold the bakery and bought a little grocery store, easier to manage I suppose. It wasn't like the bakery...but for him, not having anyone around to bake bread for or cakes," she reached for my hand, "he always asked how your sweet tooth was."

I kept thinking about the bakery, where so many memories had been lived. And as a little girl of eight, eating that cake – that memory is like it was yesterday – boy, and how I had enjoyed that cake. I looked at Mom and said, "I need a baby, Mom, but I can't have one."

She touched my arms, "then let's see if we can adopt one for you."

After wrapping up Grandpa's affairs, Mom and I boarded the long train ride home. She would now and then talk about Grandpa, but ever increasing, she talked about me having a baby. "One that could play with George. And Gracie, I'd like to be a Grandma, I truly would."

I'm not glad that we had to take the trip, but I am glad that Mom asked me to be with her, as it started some mending between us. We got to spend time together that we hadn't in years. I looked upon Mom as a woman who went through hell when dad died, made her way back and married a truly wonderful man. I wonder, at her age, if she should have had Jeanette and George, but then, her home was stable and it truly made her happy. Was I jealous? Of what, that she had two children that I couldn't have? No, I just wanted Mom to enjoy her life, and it seemed that she was.

Getting back to Centralia, I stayed a few days to rest and, to be honest, I didn't want to leave Mom. One night while sitting around the dining room table, George walked in and said, "Gracie I'm thinking about getting a new car and, well, Mary and I think you should have the '41 Chevy Coupe."

I didn't see that one coming. "That's truly nice of you, but you both know I can't drive?"

Mom reached over and said, "I think you'd better start."

So, they brought the car over to Morton and before you know it, I was the proud owner of the tan '41 Chevy (something good came out of that year, right?) and true to his word, he did buy a new car -a '47 Lincoln Continental.

Leo was beside himself, "what in the hell?"
I made sure that George had only put my name on the registration. "Leo, I own it, it's mine and until I learn to drive, it's sitting right there." No way in hell was I going to have Leo get drunk and wreck my car.
The next day, I went over to Fairhart's Department store and there was Melverna and her sister-in-law Mable Fairhart. I told them what had happened.
They were ecstatic, "A new car?"
"Not that new, but yes, and (which I strongly emphasized) there is not a scratch on it. Girls, would you go with me to the high school and between the three of us, we'll get the Driver's Ed teacher to teach us how to drive." Lo and behold he accepted.
Okay, I am not going to say the first day behind the wheel was magic, I was scared, but boy, was a hell of a lot of fun.

After the lesson we all went over to Red's to celebrate. After being served our 'drinks', which consisted of nothing more than Coca-Cola, I stood up and said, "ladies, if you want to do something - you've got to learn to do it right and have the best teacher or information to do it."
Mabel and Melverna just began to laugh, "Gracie, with you around, we're going to get into a whole lot of trouble."
I looked at them and said, "and that is a bad thing?"

I wasn't the only person the family wondered about. George Sr. appeared on the page 1 of the Daily Olympian – June 29th - which had a headline that read:
Olympian Sees Flying Discs
Another flying saucer report was made Saturday. George Barner, State Supervisor of Savings and Loan, who lives at 820

Fifth Avenue West, said he saw the mysterious aerial objects late Thursday afternoon in the direction of Mount Rainier.

Now, at least I have never claimed about seeing flying saucers; other things maybe, but never flying saucers and never in print!

Many a spirit was lifted when in early October, the moratorium on the Loggers' celebration was lifted. God bless Ross Surnworth, he turned it into an event, but a crazy name, 'Timber Wolves Daze'. Why? No one seemed to know, or get it, but it happened and that we were proud of. He worked his tail off getting bleachers built, and during the event there was high climbing on trees near the Tilton River, cable splicing and tie loading as well as something even more exciting, power saws were seen and heard.

Leo was back into helping, as this is one event that drinking was definitely encouraged.

I don't know why, but the winter of '47 wasn't as bad as the past five. Maybe the self-help books were working or was it when I found out I could take creative writing courses through the mail. I don't know, but that started helping a lot.

Oh, it wasn't just the creative writing courses you could get through the mail, but also courses in hypnotism. This definitely got me a bit excited. I did find it hard to practice on myself – you need a partner and I wasn't going to tell Leo what I was doing. He would have thought that an insane asylum would be my next home.

I also stated getting joy putting little cherubs all around the house, one for every baby I had lost; for some reason that comforted me that year and each year ever since.

I think I also found a new way to find friends and not be alone in the house, and that was the fact that I started joining groups like mad.

The only problem I had being around the 'ladies groups' such as the Methodist Church, The Eastern Star, The Daughters of the Nile and even the Lutheran Church were that, at every meeting it seemed like the talk always ended up around pickles and pregnancy, and since I wasn't about to get pregnant anytime soon, that was not the conversation I was looking for.
God only knows why I'd want to join more churches than just one, ones I didn't even go to, except the women I loved hanging around with went there.

If I wasn't at a lady's function, there was also the waiting around for Leo to either come home from working in the woods or going out in the woods to hunt wild game. Which when he brought it home, what was I to do? Be the dutiful wife and help clean, cut and package it, and of course eat it.

I also learned to can some of that game as well as fruits and vegetables - you see, as I've said, winters weren't easy in this part of the world, and with not a lot of money, the pantry became a good friend at meal time. Living in that house was miserable. First it was small and second, it was c-o-l-d. There was just a small wood stove that you had to stoke – no heater, just the small wood stove. And when your bones are frozen all the way through, a small wood stove takes forever and sometimes never to thaw your bones out.

The holidays didn't pass as quickly as I had hoped, but on New Year's Eve when Leo kissed me, I pulled back and said, "Leo, my new year's resolution is to have a child."
He looked at me and thought I had gone mad, "You are going to try for another one?"
"Nope, I'm not crazy. I've been reading about adoptions and I think we can do this."

Now, I want you to know that I'm not religious, or superstitious, but *just for good measure* I put a mustard seed in some plastic and tied it to my wrist watch. I know you are going to say, "well, the Bible says something like, 'If you have faith the size of a mustard seed, nothing will be impossible for you.' I know that's not the exact wording, but here I am quoting the Bible. That might be first and last time for that. Lord.

I didn't realize how hard it was to adopt. First, where do you begin to find out about adoptions? Thankfully, Mom was there to help. She understood my dilemma. Through contacts in Seattle, both she and George opened many doors that I couldn't do from Morton. And in my life came this miracle. But, I'm jumping ahead. You see, there are a lot of hoops you have to jump through, over and under before you can adopt. The first thing asked is, "why do you want a baby?" Without missing a beat, I gave everyone and anyone who would listen to me the story I didn't want to tell, but that said, I only stated that there were three births, not all the ones that actually happened. Besides, would anyone believe me?

Then the paperwork, the money, more paperwork and the waiting. I didn't really care if we were to adopt a newborn or one that was a few months old, but I was hoping for that. And, the one thing I didn't do was tell anyone except Esther. She could keep a secret. Just like all the babies that had died, what would happen if everyone found out and then an adoption wouldn't or couldn't take place? This ate at the deepest part of my soul. I don't know exactly how it happened, but I remember making my way with Leo to the court house, to fill out papers as we were going to be given the opportunity, and I remember the judge saying that to us, 'an opportunity to adopt' a baby born on May 4th.

I could not believe it when I was told this. Me, Gracie. I was going to be able to be a mother, and have a baby. The judge smiled at us, and after agreeing that 'all the paperwork was in order', we signed above our typed names and then the doors of the chambers opened and there stood a woman holding this little baby.

"Leo and Mrs. Hansen, meet your son."

I about fainted. How many times had I wanted those words to be spoken? She slowly walked over and gently placed this little baby, this amazing gift into my arms. All I could do is whisper, 'thank you.'

Leo wrapped his arms around me and I could feel the pressure of his chest against my back. "We can take him home?"

The judge was very caring, "Yes, the adoption is complete, he's yours."

"Hi, Sam."

Leo pulled my arm back, "Grace."

"No one will ever know that he wasn't the first – I really need to honor my daddy."

Slowly we made our way down the hallway, out to the car and on the way to our little home in Morton, never once letting him out of my arms. Here was this three-week-old, nestled in my arms as if he was meant to be there. And, honestly, the moment I held him, he too knew he was meant to be there.

I found my mouth whisper, 'thank you.' Was that to God? I think it was to every baby that hadn't lived, every second I cried and feared the worse, to every emotion I had that I now could let go of, I was holding a gift that meant more than any amount of money could.

Leo couldn't contain himself either. He went out to celebrate, and to be honest, this time I didn't care. I was happy being in our home with our baby. Esther stopped over when she heard the news. After fussing over him, she turned to me, "What's his name?"

"Sam Hansen."

"Gracie, that was..."

"I know, but as I told Leo, no one will ever know about my first Sam. This one will be given the love of two children. I'll probably smother him, give him too much of everything and he might, what some say spoiled. But, he's mine."

Esther held out her arms to hold him, "Come here, little Sammie, come to Aunt Esther."

When I placed him in her arms, she smiled at me, "I'm pregnant almost six months."

"But you're not showing."

"He, because I know it's a boy, he's sitting really far on my backbone, it hurts, but we'll get through it."

"And Sambo will be his friend?"

"Wouldn't want it any other way."

And the next morning I called Mom and George and that weekend they came over to join in on the celebration with Jeanette and George in tow. As I was fixing dinner, Mom walked into the kitchen, put her arms around me and hugged me tight. I needed that, maybe more now than ever. It was the 'all right' that I used to get from Daddy – and 'all rights' don't come around very much in my life.

My life. It changed, yes, you will say, it should have, but I mean *really* changed. I was no more a dumpy housewife with a husband who drank more than he brought home, no, I was Gracie Hansen with a baby. And those who didn't talk to me much, would now stop by to want to take a look at my little Sambo. I know that's not how you gain friends, but if I was going to be Mrs. Leo Hansen in Morton, I knew I had to be more than stuck in a small shack reading self-help books and feeling depressed.

And with that, I felt like I had enough courage to also do something that I had put off for about two years – mail in an article that I had written – sent it into a small magazine, Boot and Shoe Recorder. Not too fancy, right? Well, doll, you have to start somewhere and, I figured after reading about their acceptance of articles from new author I thought I'd give it a try. And lo and behold, not over three weeks later I get a letter in the mail saying that they would publish my article! ME! A published author! The letter stated that I would get $26.00 for the article sent in, and if I had anymore they would entertain looking at them as well. I didn't. I stopped while the going was good. With such quick success for the first time out, I didn't want to spoil any 'beginner's luck' – nope. I put my pen away and didn't write another line, not for a long time.

My life as a mom was more important. This was my final try at being a mom, and since this one was alive, kicking and sometimes crying, I felt that I should keep my focus on one area of doing something right at a time. I'm going to tell you this and I don't know if any other mother feels this, but for the first year or so, all I could focus on was Sambo.

Now, the good lord and everyone else will tell you that I am not the best housekeeper, but I can cook like nobody's business and I believe one can outweigh the other, right? I mean, a full belly is much better than a bed that is made. Yes, I know, I was raised to make my bed, but now it didn't seem like that much of a deal. I wanted to make Sambo's first Easter, first 4th of July, first Jamboree, first Halloween, first Thanksgiving, first Christmas and, within that year his first birthday as well, experiences neither of us could forget.

It was hard, too. I like staying busy and Sambo kept me busy. But, my mind started to turn cloudy and sad, even with this wonderful bundle. Because through all the first was also first tooth, first step, first...you get my drift. And, I will say this, and please don't get the wrong impression, but as Sambo grew, Leo stayed away more. Was this child just for me? It seemed that way. Now, I will say that I did make a point in not allowing liquor to be around Sambo, at all. I was subjected to that enough and now that a new life was in the house, the liquor either had to stay under control or stop all together. Knowing Leo, that was a tall order, but he did try. But, what was he to do with a small baby? It didn't want to hunt or fish, right? And, well, logging at this point was well out of the question. Leo stayed away. I got depressed and Sambo must have felt it. You don't get do-over's with your children, but I want to say that not having many skills in the mother department, I wasn't that terrible.

Sambo's year two was a bit more challenging than year one. But he, for the most part, was just like any two-year-old – growing up.
It wasn't until he was three that I felt that I should go out and find some work to supplement Leo's wages. Loading up Sambo in the car, I headed back up to Red's Café. I didn't really quit last time, so I had taken a long leave of absence – of three years. I walked in and Melverna was wiping down the counter and looked over at me. "With that look on your face, I think you are wanting your old job back."
"Tall order, isn't it?"
"You are welcome here anytime, and since our girl we hired is leaving for camp in a couple weeks, we'd love to have someone who knows their way around. But Grace, what about Sambo?"
"If I get the job, that will work itself out as well." I didn't know how, putting the cart before the horse was something I was good at, so, why not now? So, I was to start on Monday, reduced hours from before but it was a couple extra dollars that wasn't coming in now. And it just so happened that Jeanette wanted to come visit for awhile. I talked it over with both Mom and Jeanette and they both agreed that this would give her

some responsibilities and with a couple coins her way, it sweetened the pie a bit.

Since Jeanette couldn't drive, she pushed Sambo up to the restaurant in the stroller. Now, I know he was three and a bit too big for the stroller, but this way she could keep track of him. That summer, my hours were pretty solid, but as school started, and Jeanette left, they were dropped down to almost nothing. But, by then, I knew there was something else Leo and Gracie would have to do, find a bigger house. And we did.

We couldn't move in until after the first of the year, but what a difference when we did. Sambo screamed with delight and, well, so did I! There was enough room for Sambos to have a proper bedroom. It wasn't a crammed corner made out to be a room. And I felt like I had 'stepped up' in the world. No longer was I cooking on a little wood stove, now I had appliances and stairs that led up to my house and room.

1952 felt like a good year. Until. I know. The shoe always drops doesn't it? While I'm at Red's I get a call from Esther, "Mike's wife is in the hospital, and it sounds serious!" And it was by Sunday she died, suddenly, of boulder polio. I've never heard of it, but we were all shocked. Here was this mother of two, working at the store, helping Mike fill orders for delivery and then dead - Fairhart's Department Store will never be the same. I didn't like the feeling when I drove into Morton all those years ago and the first thing past the 'Welcome to Morton' sign is the graveyard. That's gotta say something, right?

When I got home I ran over and hugged Sambo – never had I been so happy to see his face, feel his arms around my neck. "Mommy's crying."

"I'm just so glad to see you." And that was no lie. I had faced death many times in my years, Grandpa and Grandma, my dad, the babies, those all were hard, but now having someone close to my age die – it stung.

Just that morning, after I heard the news, I called Helen Tregoing, Trig is what we called her for short. She owned one of the taverns in town and a place where I might find Leo. But, this time it wasn't about finding the husband, this time it was finding someone to talk to. I was going to see Esther, but she was pretty shook up herself. Helen watched me bring Sambo into the tavern and invited me over to one of the tables near the rear. "You can smoke, Sambo can eat some french-fries and you and I can talk." Exactly what I needed. She only served Pepsi, so I obliged to drink it – there is a difference between Coke and Pepsi, but when it's served free, there are no complaints – or there shouldn't be.

About that time, I started feeling like time was ticking too fast, and there was nothing I could do to slow it down. You see your time go by when you have children. There's a bench mark of things that happen and like it or not, you either get off the pot or squat for dear life. So, I got up off the pot, or should I say the couch, went down to Red's and turned my apron in. I hadn't done that before, but this time, it felt right. Sambo was in preschool and well, I couldn't sit around a restaurant counter forever. Closing the door at Red's I looked up and down the street. Now what, Gracie?

I walked over to the State Bank of Morton, talked to Ross Dill and asked for a job. There was no application to fill out, as they all kind of knew me from me serving their lunches. What better way to get in people's faces, right?

Well, I don't know if it was the 'right' job for me, but at the time, it felt right. Getting dressed up, looking at people's bank accounts and getting to chat sitting down – all the time getting paid for it. I felt pretty lucky. And after awhile I began to feel better about my choice.

I began to feel less depressed and with a little extra money, I went out to Fairhart's Department Store and made a deposit on a Singer Featherweight sewing machine which I had touched, tested out and knew I wanted just that machine. Mike told me it was one of the best machines for the money, "and if you need to, you can make weekly payments to help out as well."

I had never bought anything on time, and now I felt I was becoming a modern, independent woman – sold! While coming in each week, I also looked over the cloth choices. Would figure out what would look good as a dress, scarf or a jacket and then go home and sketch out from memory what I had seen in a magazine from the bank. Leo would come in and look at the disaster, as he'd call it and say, "woman, you can't sew and live in the living room at the same time." Silently, I agreed. But, I'd stay on my hands and knees cutting out a pattern that I designed using newspaper.

With my last payment, I loaded the machine in the car and drove right home. God, I loved the machine. I look back on it now and realize that, that machine was my very first major purchase ever, and a damn good one at that. That thing lasted through one marriage, a lot of life's changes and many dresses! And I still use it to this day

I felt like a new woman. Working at the bank, I began to socialize more and that's when Esther asked if I wanted to join the PTA. Since Sambo would be going to first grade next year, I thought I'd better start getting involved now.
At one of the meetings it was discussed how 'funds were low' and 'isn't there some way to do a special event.'

That night I chatted with Esther and told her what I had done in Centralia, the 'experience' of putting on small skits in the garage and how, to my amazement, people paid to come see them. Esther thought that it was worth a shot, so for the next meeting, I prepared an outline of an idea, 'let's use local talent and put on a talent show.' It was enthusiastically received and before you knew it, I was the chair of the fundraising committee and began working on the first ever what was to be known as 'Morton Follies'.

This was exactly what I needed. I'd talk to the customers at the bank, they in turn would tell someone else, and then pretty soon I had a list of potential people to perform, alongside the members of the PTA.

One day Esther walked me home and asked a question that I hadn't really thought out, "so what is going to be performed?" I smiled and said, "I'm getting a few ideas together." Which I had begun to jot down but soon I gathered people together, and by the time opening night arrived I had written, cast, staged and once or twice stood on the stage and performed. In the program I made them put, *'Written, Borrowed, Stolen, Directed, and Produced by Gracie Hansen.'* Best advertising I didn't have to pay for. It was a typical variety show using all the home talent. Most of the time we had a hundred people in the cast. Everybody's got a little bit of ham in them! And geez, those people would just get up there and give the most terrific performances. They were wonderful. We had a chorus line, ten of the young housewives. (I think one time we figured out that they had about 26 children between them). I would get a dancing teacher to teach them how to dance and they worked real hard and they were terrific. It was thrilling. Tickets were sold, people came, but one thing I learned, to get people to come, you had to cast members of their families. Then more people would come.

I went over to the local newspaper and talked up the show. They came to one of the rehearsals and took several photos, interviewed me, and lo and behold, in a couple of days, there we were on the front page. Not with one photo but with two! (and one had me in it!) And I was being quoted! And by the time the closing curtain happened on our second night we had raised over $1,000!

The committee was ecstatic and begged me to continue as the fund-raising chair person. SO, for six solid years I was, as I call it, the ringleader for the Morton Follies. What a blast that was. Esther and Reg, her husband, had just moved from their little home next to their car dealership and had a stylish country home built for them. She demanded, and after seeing the house, I could not <u>not</u> have the closing party at their new home.

Everyone laughed, drank and ate until we couldn't stay up any longer. I knew right then that I had found my calling. Wading through being a housewife, a waitress and now a bank teller, I knew what I needed to do. I needed to follow my passion of theatre – the Morton Follies wasn't just a one year, two night event.

The odd thing was, the town became closer to being the entertainment center of Lewis County; with having the Morton Follies becoming such an event, and the ever increasing Loggers' Jubilee, people were not only heading to visit Mt. St Helens or Mt. Rainier, but they were also coming to Morton and staying for a day or two. Soon the town was given the title of "The Tie Mill Capital of the World". This meant that it had the longest railroad tie dock in the world, which supplied railroad ties for all of the United States and some say was responsible for most of the remaining railroad ties for the Burmese Railroad. I was told that I should watch the movie *Bridge on the River Kwai*. I asked why, and they said it showed the history of the amazing journey for the Burmese Railroad to be built and finished. So I finally did. The one thing I wasn't told, Morton isn't mentioned once. Good movie, Alec Guinness is wonderful, but it didn't help to let people know just how much involvement our little town had in the building of the railroad.

During this time Carl had graduated from Law School, was a claims adjuster (just for a bit), and then set up practice in Spokane. Can I tell you just how proud I am of my baby brother? Lord, he had gone in the military, came out a stronger man and went on to fight off the battle field for people's rights. (He helped me out a time or two also.)

I wasn't the only one 'going into showbizness'. On the front page of The Morton Journal, with other children parading around, was Sambo – *'Chorus Line in Year(s) To Come' (April 1, 1954).*

And, not to be outdone by being in the papers, Mom too started getting some notice. It read:

New Proprietor For Gift Shop Here – January 28, 1954 -Mary Barner's Gift Shop is the new name of the former Haskin's Gift Shop at 1057 Capitol Way which was purchased recently by Mrs. George Barner. A wide variety of gift items will be offered, Mrs. Barner announced, including costume jewelry, glassware, gift cards and wrappings, stationery and school supplies, stockings, gloves and handbags. A new stock of merchandise to supplement present supplies will arrive shortly.

Now, Mom had been the Manager of Empire Beauty Shoppe in Longview (Mezzanine Floor, Empire Drug No. 2 'For Precious Little Aids in Beauty'). I love that...but moving to Olympia seems to have brought her uptown. I was happy to see that she was going to carry costume jewelry – something every woman, especially this gal, needed. (do I hear an amen?)

Things were certainly changing around here. The Follies was put on for the second year and it was bigger than the first and a lot harder. I guess 'cause people expected more than what they got the first time. I would. We still got front page with several photos, but now it seemed that the PTA wanted to raise money for almost anything – the Follies was a hit and I was the one that made it happen.

And like I said, even the Loggers' Jubilee had to make improvements. There were permanent concrete bleachers constructed by Grose Construction Co. of Morton, new concession stands, a portable all-purpose building, a Queen's contest to advertise Jubilee (the first queen was Kathy Boren crowned this year, 1954), and the first Jubilee float built (built under the direction of Chamber President Jerry Mullins and Don Gayman). Was Morton hitting the big time or what?

Our Follies must have been more than a hit last year, as the paper started putting things out early, like this article:

Plans Put In Motion For Another Big PTA Vaudeville.

Strange things will be happening from now until Nov 18 and 19 when the Morton PTA presents its second annual mammoth vaudeville revue. (mammoth? To me, those are big words and big shoes to fill!)

This year's show will be under the direction of Gracie Hansen, who promises the 1954 revue will be a riot of gaiety and laughter starring the best local talent.
Thursday, Oct 14, at 8 p.m. the first organizational meeting will be held in the grade school lunch room. All who are interested are asked to be there so things can start rolling.

Mrs. Hansen urges anyone interested in participating in any way to contact her before that date. Mrs. Hansen feels fortunate in having the assistance this year of J. J. Johnson, local speech teacher, who has had professional experience in theatre work both in New York summer stock and in California. He will be the producer of the show.

Last year's show was a smash hit and highly successful from all standpoints. All profits from this community affair go to the PTA for use in projects to aid the school children. You do not have to sing or dance or play a horn to participate. Just contact Gracie Hansen, phone 3919 and you'll be surprised what you can do.

And the phone rang. Yes, by then we had our own phone. And where were answering machines when you needed them? J.J. Johnson was named as producer, but as a producer, he should have also taken some of the calls! And can you believe they actually put phone numbers in the paper?

It all started coming together and then I realized that there were some people that should be on that stage that weren't on my list. One was Ross Dill. So I went into his office and said, "Hey, since you always have your nose stuck in papers, how about if you come and be part of the Follies and see what fun you have been missing."

And without batting an eye, he replied, "I was waiting for the invitation."

Right then, I learned one important rule: always ask. You might be turned down, but you will never know until you ask.

My popularity grew at the bank. I wasn't just 'Gracie Hansen, first teller'; nope, I was 'Gracie Hansen, the go-to-girl.'

I need to let you know, the more you get, the more is asked of you. Last year was an adventure, seeing IF I could do it, but this year was more, 'let's get it done'. Even with J. J. around it was still pretty much my show. He would give pointers on how things are supposed to happen. I was grateful he was around, but he was needed a bit more than he thought he should have been. And to make things bigger we had larger acts. Here, let me give you the details of the review (yes, this thing got reviewed!)

Good Crowd Out For Morton Follies

"The Morton Follies of 1954" presented Thursday and Friday nights clicked again this year. The gymnasium was packed each night by an appreciative audience.

It was generally agreed that Gene Johnson, the versatile young man about town, just about stole the show representing a woman of Morton. Also his wrestling bout with Eugene Bingaman, the "Masked Marvel" was another act well received.

Mrs. Teckla Johnson and Mrs. Grave Bradley put on the "Clam Digger's Sweetheart" in an act where the costumes alone were good for a laugh. Jack Mires represented Sally Rand. One in the audience was heard to ask if Jack had been to Copenhagen.

One is led to wonder if the women dancing the Charleston can kick now the way they did, what would it have been 25 years ago. Les Ingerson and Herschel Wilson, Jr. shot each other in "The Killing of Dan McGrew." With Dan McGrew popular with the dance hall girls.

All the acts were good, some just a bit better than others. The show was directed by Mrs. Gracie Hansen, assisted by J. J. Johnson of the school faculty. Following the Friday night show the cast held a party for the participants, their wives and husbands in the VFW hall.

And remember, this was right between Halloween and Thanksgiving! Again the show did really well for the PTA, for the school kids and for me. I didn't have too much time to plan for Christmas as the 1955 Follies was right around the corner!

I probably forgot to include Leo in all of this. During most of the past several years, our marriage, well, wasn't a marriage. It was a war zone. Oh, not in front of Sambo, if I could help it. But, with anything, if it grabs a hold you generally cannot shake it by yourself. Leo's best friend was alcohol. In fact, I used to say it was the last thing he had on his mind when he went to sleep and the first thing on his mind when he woke. Sure, he worked his hours as a logger and he did hunt and fish and brought home food for the table, but a building has to have more parts that just four walls and a roof, and Leo seemed to think that was all there was to it.

I thought that if I cast him in the Follies he'd see that I was trying to pull him into things that interested me. I knew the canning, sewing and PTA wasn't his thing. And sure enough, he took to it like a fish to water. But once the applause was over, back to the bottle he went. As with most things, I told myself, it'll get better. But it didn't. And I knew that was going to have to change. But right when I was getting my courage up, in came a request for me to be the emcee at various functions and fundraisers; fundraisers for local political events. You could have bowled me over. What? Me? But, without much hesitation, I went out and started raising points and dollars for the power folks.

This working at the bank, trying to be a mom to Sambo, and the PTA Follies, my life was finally going in full stride. Morton didn't look as gloomy as it had. The '55 Follies went off without a hitch and so did the '56 Follies. I was proud that all this hard work was going to something. In '56 the Follies were put on around Easter so there was some fun adding Peter Cottontail for the kids, and our goal this year was to raise enough money to build a play shed for the grade school.

And, because it was a political year, I was asked to take the Follies on the road. I don't think anyone believed this at first, but there were everyday Morton folks on stage with various political hopefuls. We traveled to Centralia, Longview and, before you knew it, we were playing at the Shriner's in Tacoma!

I have to laugh now, this little show that was first done to raise money for schools was now being used to help raise money for officials. That's what gave me the idea, and after some talks with Carl, my brother and now lawyer, I started a little company, 'Gracie Hansen's Enterprises, Inc'. I had business cards printed and every chance I got, I handed them out. This may be the ticket out of Morton. The cards read "bar supplies – special entertainment – complete insurance-show productions".

I didn't know what I was doing really, but did I when the Follies started, and now look?

And, Carl could have told me I was crazy, but he helped me anyway.

Esther knew if I wasn't at the bank or at a PTA or Follies meeting, I'd be sitting at my sewing machine. So that's where she found me to show me what she had cut out from a local magazine. "Looks like you are not the only one who likes to make news!"

She was right. There in the photo was George Sr. with pen in hand and several people standing around him. The headline read:

Celebrating our Heritage, Embracing our Future. July 17, 1957. George Barner, State Supervisor of Savings and Loan Associations, signs the articles of incorporation for the Washington State Employees Local 443 Credit Union

It looked mighty official. Now I bet you are going to say, 'with a stepfather in high offices, a mother who seems to be graced with beauty and who is in the society column a lot, I would get special treatment.' Let me tell you, no doors opened for me because of this. Remember, my name isn't Barner and I wasn't even close to the State Capitol...Morton is a place where people forget you, and I was going to try and change all that.

For the next few months, I learned a valuable word – strategize.

Jumping a bit ahead, but this is where it started, I took a course on effective speaking, and on June 2, 1958, I received my diploma from the Dale Carnegie Courses. When I had a place to display it prominently, I did. It reads: *Dale Carnegie Courses – This certifies that Gracie Hansen has successfully completed the Dale Carnegie Course in Effective Leadership Training and Human Relations*. Now, I know it wasn't the Junior College Diploma that Mom was hoping for, but it was an accomplishment for me and also another notch in my belt that showed "Gracie was serious!"

When I heard that Mike Fairhart secretly married a girl by the name of Mitzi I was ecstatic. Okay, so maybe there is hope to find love after such a devastation as losing someone he cared so much for. She was 16 years his junior, but you know, when I heard that I said, "he's going to have some fun after all that pain!" And, was I right. In no time a little Fairhart was added, making their home three, and within another year there would be another. I then thought, if it can happen to such a great guy as Mike, it just might happen to an okay woman like Gracie; either Leo had to become like Mike or I had to find someone like Mitzi – my mind was made up.

I don't know how or why, but 1957 was like a wind of change for me. It could have been that the Follies had opened doors that I had so long wanted open, or it could have been just me, wanting to dare myself with new things. But there was one thing I was on sound ground about, Leo was no longer going to be anything in my life. Sambo and I could do it on our own; hadn't we really lately anyway? Here was my little boy, turning nine and me? A girl never tells her age after a certain point-but honey, I had matured.

And, this year's Follies were going to be the last for the PTA. It seemed ripe, like an apple, to take it to a larger stage. Hell, hadn't we been a hit in Tacoma, Centralia and Longview? I know those aren't such big cities, but the real point is, outside Morton the audience loved the show just the same. I overheard someone talking one day, "She makes people do normally what the wouldn't do and they're good!" In a way, I was the 'It Girl'. I found the 'it' that I was good at! So, after staging this year's, I was going to figure a way to move it away from the PTA.

What seemed like too much fate smiling down on me, an opportunity came knocking at my door.

You take opportunities that are given to you, am I not right? Well, this one is a bit odd, you might say, especially since I was having a lot of problems with Leo being influenced by the bottle. I was presented the opportunity of running the Morton Liquor Store. You are going to say, and so did I, 'this is a bit out of left field,' right? I had to look at it with a couple thoughts in mind ~~starting with the job~~ was a Civil Service gig.

It was steady employment + it

Some said I was a shoe-in, especially because of all the extra work I was doing for the political arena, but I need to tell you, yes, it's nice to know some top honchos, but you still have to go through an application process to be appointed, you don't buy into the store like other states. Nope, all the liquor is controlled by the State, for the State. And, fortunate for me, George's brother Don was operating one in Centralia for awhile, so if I did have questions, I had someone I could trust to help guide me, if needed. You might remember, he was the man I mentioned when Michael was fighting for his life? He worked for a while as Centralia's Fire Chief.

So I put my hat in the ring to get the liquor license. It would take months of processes, background checks and of course, maybe trying to find out why anyone would be fool enough to leave the bank to run a liquor store, but that's what I was aiming to do.

With the license up, so was the lease on the space for the store, so whoever got the license also got to set up a new store. Now, I don't hesitate to take on a challenge, and this one was right up my alley.

All of '57 was getting all my ducks in a row. And by the time December rolled around, I received the Christmas present I thought was going to solve all my problems – I got approval to run the store! And some truly believe I got the liquor store partially because of my 'numerous whirlwind political campaigns' for the Democratic candidates in Lewis County. I am hoping it was because I was the best broad for the job.

The ironic thing about my life is how some things run parallel. In The Daily Chronicler there were two articles on the same page-side-by-side, mentioning me. Here goes...you're going to love this.

December 6, 1957 New Liquor Manager Mrs. Grace Hanson has been named to take over the operation of the Morton liquor store. She will officially start Monday. The store will be moved from its present location in the Gross building to the old music store, or Dill building, on west Main street.

AND

Big Crowd at PTA Meeting MORTON — The Morton Parent Teacher association met In the multi- purpose room of the new high school Monday night, with a record crowd in attendance...which was opened by the flag salute by the assemblage, followed by the invocation by the Rev. Everette M. Filbert of the Methodist church. Mrs. Leo Hansen, ways and means chairman, reported the committee had decided to withdraw the "Follies" as a potential project this year. She said another local organization had requested the sponsorship of the show....it was voted to have a carnival as the money making project this season, and an athletic dinner next fall, with all interested invited to attend. The dinner is not intended as a moneymaker, but merely a social evening to promote good fellowship in the community.

Okay, here goes. Did you notice that for the liquor store story my name was Mrs. Grace Hanson (on) and for the PTA article my name was Mrs. Leo Hansen (en); same person, same page, different spellings. So not to confuse people? I'm still confused when I read it. Guess they didn't want people to get the PTA mixed up with the liquor store...well, sweetie, liquor and the PTA will have something in common soon!

Right after the liquor store moved and it was set up, I made my move.

Now, like I said, for quite awhile things hadn't been good between Leo and myself. I can count on one hand the 'good years' in the last seventeen with Leo. As I was setting up the store, I noticed the 'extra room' in the back and thought, 'hell, Gracie, all you would have to do is put on your clothes and walk ten feet to work." And it was right then I made up my mind, Leo can have whatever life he wants, but Gracie is going to move out and move on.

Leo was excited that old Gracie here was going to have access to liquor, and I told him before he opened his mouth that he had to think of it like anything else. "If it's for sale and you want some, you gotta pay for it."

So, I walked in the living room and said, "Leo, I'm moving out."

He stood up and said, "Oh, think you are so high and mighty now, huh?"

And I looked at him and thought, it's not worth it but said, "Nope, I'm just done." Turned around, picked up my purse, yelled at Sambo to follow me, and headed toward the door. Now, I knew that I wouldn't get out the door without a fight. The fight wouldn't be about me or the marriage, naw, it was about a woman walking out on Leo – any woman.

He made his way to the door and tried to block it.

"It's all right Leo. You can stand there and stop me now, but you go to work tomorrow and I will be gone when you get back home. So, it's either you let us leave now, or you wait until tomorrow, but it's going to happen."

He stepped back and said, "this is not worth a fight. Get out and never come back."

Sambo walked past us and out the door, and when I knew he was safe, I too walked out the door and said, "I'll be back, but just to get some of the stuff, the rest is all yours."

In the car I told Sambo, "You gotta do what is right for you no matter what, and son, this is so right for both of us."

Christmas was small, but thank goodness for friends. Sambo and I didn't have to spend time in the back room of the liquor store. Now, the house we left was a big house, and what we had now, well let me describe it for you. There were two large rooms with cement floors. It certainly wasn't built for anyone to live there, but with a couple bits of furniture, we were going to have a home. I had stepped backwards on the living arrangement department, but miles ahead on living.

Trying to get the Follies up and running, as well as watching the store full-time, just wasn't working. Fortunately, I found a high school girl to help out when needed. I know, I hired a high school girl to work at the liquor store. Sounds crazy? Well, yes and no. She was smart, dependable, Sambo and I adored her, and no one seemed to mind. It actually worked out really well. She lived with us full-time and this kept her on track to finish high school, because she probably wouldn't have ~~because of~~ *otherwise* problems at home, and it allowed me to have someone to watch after the store and Sambo.

And *is* a good thing I did. You know, just when you think you are on a roll, the ball rolls over you!

Just when I was going to open the store, I started feeling queasy and as I was headed to the bathroom I felt something horrible begin to jab inside of me. 'I can't be having a miscarriage, you have to have sex for that...' and before I knew it, I was asking for help and soon rushed to the hospital. No sooner had I gotten into a room then I was then rushed to Olympia. I kept asking, "What about Sambo?" God bless friends like Esther and Melverna. He was in good hands and I was getting prepped for surgery. That's right, the best they could figure out, I had a blockage or something and I needed to be operated on right away.
"Are you sure it's not my appendix or a miscarriage?"
The doctor looked down at me and smiled, "Miss, both of those I am sure it is not."

During the long surgery I lost a lot of blood, and ~~they~~ *everyone* started getting worried that I wouldn't make it. They didn't

know the fighter they had in this ole gal, right? Well, by the time I found my bearings, there stood Mom and George. She had this horrible look on her face and the instant she saw my eyes open up I could have sworn I saw tears. "Gracie, you're with us!"
I could hardly speak, but I wanted to say, 'where in the hell else would I be?' Those words wouldn't come as I quickly fell back to sleep.

I would learn later that I was in the hospital for almost a week and, would you believe this, I had a tumor. Ovarian cancer. When I heard this, I started to laugh. No one could see the joke in it. I could and still can – after attempting to give birth to all those babies who died and now cancer of the ovary! Take it out and get rid of it, it was worthless anyway. What I also learned was that I was very lucky to have the warning signs that I did, as if it had gone on much longer, I probably would have died. And then I wouldn't get to tell you the rest of my story, now, would I?

When you get a wake-up call like that, you better answer it. When they finally got me back to the store, I was in bad shape. It took a long time to get back to a bit of normal. Thank goodness for Sambo and my little high school girl, or else I would be dead. Alongside my friends and family, they were my constant.
As I lay there, I started working on Follies 1958. This was going to be the year. I've put all the tools in place and the funds from the Follies were going to be used to finance more productions. As I have always been told, 'build on your past successes and learn from your past failures.'

I began rehearsing the show in the back of the store and when I could, I'd go out and try to sell ads. In fact, I went as far as Olympia and Tacoma to see if I could get some takers.
Stopped in to Mom's shop, not only to see her and her jewelry selection, but also to see if she had an ad she wanted to place.

Business has a necessity to be resourceful and you use your resources when they are available. During our visit it was brought up I again that I wasn't the only one with showbizness in my genes. It seems that George was going to be in *Charley's Aunt* in high school, which would be on the 2nd so it wouldn't conflict with the Follies or anything. She began to laugh, "he's taking the part of the aunt. So it should be very funny, wearing a dress and wig – can you just see him?"

Well, that's what we were doing in the Follies, but seeing George dressing up in a wig and dress was something I would pay to see.

Boy, was it. We had a great time laughing and watching George parade around on stage. He didn't know, but at that moment I thought, 'now this is an audition if the Follies takes off – George can be part of the act!'

Getting home, I only had a couple weeks, as the Follies were scheduled for two nights on the 25th and 26th and there was a lot to do. Everything was going pretty good. A couple mis-steps during rehearsal, but by the time the show opened I felt that I had something that could be taken on the road. Friday's audience loved the show. Yes, there were a couple lines that went above and beyond where the show used to be, but, I needed to reach that broader audience. It wasn't until Saturday night that, well, here goes.

First, let me say that I'll admit that the dialog got racier this year, but I still kept it clean and professional. As you are aware, I hire those who want to be on stage and who are generally amateurs.

Anyway, close to the end of the show, I had arranged to have six loggers dressed up in dresses and wigs (as I had seen in *Charley's Aunt* and had done in other Follies). How it was directed and scripted was that five of the men would do the skit, then get into the Can-Can line, and then logger number six was to parade out attired as 'Queen for a Day' with the satchel and everything.

So this all happened, but when he crossed down to the edge of the stage, he hiked up his skirt and showed he had nothing on underneath but his boots! And not only that, he went into the dance line and all the loggers started doing the Can-Can, lifting their dresses up high, and they too didn't have anything on. *either* There was outrage, laughter, confusion, and I just stood in the back of the room with my mouth open. *The audience went wild*

There wasn't much rejoicing afterwards. I tried my best to put on the face of 'well, that's show business' and 'things like this happen', and what could I tell them, 'never do that again?' It was closing night.

One of the loggers came up to me to with what I thought was going to be an apology and said, "Gee whiz, Gracie I've gotta have a little bit of fortification before I can get up there and make a fool of myself."

Looking back on it, they did say some clever stuff, and I do wish I was clever enough to write some of the things they came up with. _down_

It wasn't until word spread from the churches that PTA even got involved.

Even though this was the only problem with the show for either night, the PTA felt that since their name had been associated with it for the past five years, and that many good church-going folks were in attendance, the Morton Follies by any name must cease to exist.

To make matters worse or better, depending on how you look at it, I noticed a tall, handsome man who parked right out front the store, but never came in.

At first I was a bit perturbed, as that was prime parking for my patrons. Then I watched where he headed. That was even more puzzling – he went over to the police station. The first time or two I thought, all right Mister, this better be good, but then I noticed that he seemed to do it on purpose. It was always about the same time each day, and when he'd park he'd look at himself in the mirror, then open his door and as he closed it he would slightly peer into the window, almost like he wanted me to notice him. Well, I did.

Then what I did was act like I was cleaning the shelves or soon, the windows of the store, and try to take a better peek. This certainly was a bright spot in what had become a horribly hard time. I looked down at my ring finger and realized that before anything would, could or should happen, this baby had to be taken off. I marched over to the phone and called the best attorney I knew, Carl. We had talked about it a couple of times, but this time, I knew I couldn't have a future unless I cleaned up the past. "File them suckers, brother, I'm ready for a new day."

I didn't even want child support from Leo. I felt that the less that tied us together, the better off we'd all be years from now. Anyway, Leo didn't even attempt to see Sambo that much, and it just seemed like I could stop any pain that might be in that little soul.

After hanging up the phone I walked back to the front of the store and whispered, 'keep parking there, buddy, someday I'll get to know your name, and maybe more.' Never did I know those words would come true.

You see, the Morton police chief, Orville 'Porky' Amondson (or 'Pork' as I liked to call him), was running for Lewis County Sheriff and I was asked to attend a Democratic function at Centralia's Lewis and Clark Hotel, and wouldn't you know it, that handsome man sat down right next to me. Some people have always thought there was something going on between Pork and myself. But, to be honest, when did I have time? Yes, he would flirt with me, and I, well, I am not one NOT to flirt, so I would give it back in spades. But no, Pork and I were just friends, it would or could have gone further, maybe, but we never let it happen. Now this tall, handsome man sitting next to me, well, let me just tell you, I could be in a bit of danger. I was praying he was married and I was praying that he wasn't. You see, my divorce was in the works and I certainly didn't want to fall for someone who I couldn't have. However, I married Leo when I was 19 and I hadn't felt like a school girl since then, until this very minute when I looked up and saw his eyes, then he smiled. "My name is Tom Cooper, and yours is Gracie Hansen, am I right?"

The wind was taken totally out of my sails. "How did you know?"

He began to laugh, "Pork told me. And how do I know Pork? He's invited me to be his undersheriff if he gets elected as Sheriff of Lewis County."

I started to laugh, almost uncontrollably, and without thinking I said, "so you parking outside my shop isn't an accident? You really are going to the police department?"

He smiled, "So, you have noticed me."

Right then I had to find my bearings, "Well, you are always taking up the prime parking spot for my customers."

"It's a public street and I am told anybody can park anywhere they please, if they are following the law."

To be honest, I didn't care what he said next. All I could think of was what he would look like in a police uniform. I mean, I was stepping from a logger to a cop. Gracie, stop. He might be married, but if he was then he shouldn't be flirting like this. Right then, the meeting started and I couldn't wait to hear more about him, but that wasn't to be. After the meeting he excused himself and began circulating the room and mostly around Porky.

I drove back to Morton with butterflies, wanting him to park outside the store so I could now properly go out and chat with him. But, just like everything else, it didn't happen.

Think I was a bit devastated? I was exhausted and then I started getting sick again. I was drained. And then, wouldn't you know it, I had to have another surgery. Hysterectomy.

God bless Esther Lester, she took Sambo in for a couple months to finish off the school year. Sambo didn't mind. You see, Esther's prediction came true, her baby turned out to be Sambo's best friend – Rod. Besides, a kid of ten probably would rather be with a family on a farm than stuck with a sick mom in the back of a liquor store.

I was tired, defeated and stuck in this shit hole of a building praying that someone would buy liquor. You would think that having a liquor store probably would have been a relatively thriving business. Yes, but in this boom-and-bust timber town where the economy fluctuates like the weather, it wasn't. I learned everyone's buying habits – between paydays people wanted to buy on credit, then on payday they would forget to pay you. Then I would have to chase them down before they spent their funds at the local tavern or grocery store. "My bills had to be paid too." I would tell them.

My dreams were fading as I lay there trying to heal. Depression started to set in. Depression isn't pretty. And when you are depressed that you have surgeries to pay for and that the income line of the ledger is shorter than the expenses, something has to give. It also isn't pretty when your family isn't close by. Jeanette, now married, moved over to Spokane to be closer to Carl; George was up in Olympia with Mom and George Sr. So here I was, flat on my back, flat in the pocketbook and flat to the world. Who wanted this 5'1" fat girl from Morton who flopped at being this 'girl of showbizness'. It was truly hopeless. And on top of that, when the primary election took place, with all the work that was put into trying to get the best turnout for Pork, he under-preformed and there was worry that he wouldn't make it to the general election. I put some of the blame on me. Why not? Wasn't I part of his political machine to win? I know I sound sorry for myself, 'poor me', but like I said, depression isn't fun.

Fortunately, when it came to the general election, it all seemed to turn around. Pork did win the election and, true to his word, he hired a man by the name of Tom Cooper to be his undersheriff.

Now, what I didn't know, and I should have asked even one person in the small town of Morton, Tom was a hometown boy.

But he had moved away many years ago and headed off to California where he was with the LAPD for about seven years, before moving to Oregon and then right back to Washington.

And on January 12, 1959, they were both sworn in to serve Lewis County.

Winters are hard on me. I like the sunshine and not the rain, cold, snow, wind – it's just plain miserable. And the longer the days were dark, so was my mind. I tried, lord knows I tried, to find bright spots in my world. Sambo would come home and chat about school, Esther would come over and we'd talk, but for the most part my walls were the store and they pressed against my heart until I wanted to die. One day I walked to the back of the store and sat down on the cot that was my bed. I looked up and saw water running down the walls. I threw up my hands and said, "Gracie, welcome to hell." My body couldn't find the strength from all of the depression as well as from the surgeries, hell the doctors had taken everything out but my teeth, and I bet you they wanted to do that as well. I lay back against the wall and said, "Hell IS hell."

And wouldn't you know it, my angel Esther walked into the store and right back to where I was sitting. I looked up with tears running down my cheeks and I said, "Esther, I'm ready to give up. If this is all I have to live for, I might as well."
She stood there looking down at me and said, "Well, Sambo is always welcome to come live with us."
"Foolish, right?"
"No, Gracie, it's not foolish to have dreams. Or not to get to live them the way you wanted to. But honey, when a door closes, open another one."
"Thank you for that advice, Miss School Teacher, I bet your class loves to hear that."
"They don't, and I didn't think you would either."

"Esther, look at that water running down that wall. A couple years ago I was working at a bank bringing home $277.50 a month, my son had his own room, the Follies were the highlight of the entertainment in town, and I was married. Now look at me."

Esther, god bless her, wrapped her arms around my waist and said, "Sure, let's have a pity party for Gracie. She hasn't had one in a while, and this is the best time to have one." And she leaned in and hugged me tight.

I cried and cried, until the tears couldn't come out anymore. And then Esther said, "now for new beginnings."

I wiped my face with the handkerchief that was being presented to me, and once most of the wet stuff was off my face, she handed me a newspaper. "This all seems like miles and years away, but there has been talk for several years about having something like the 1909 Alaska-Yukon-Pacific Exposition, which if done soon would be its 50th anniversary, but others are saying it should be in 1961 to celebrate the 100th anniversary of the boundary survey between Canada and the United States, and get this, they want to call it the 'Festival of the West', or 'the Pan-Pacific Age of Science Exposition', or 'the World Science Pan-Pacific Exposition'. And they want to put it either at Duwamish Head or Fort Lawton or First Hill, Midway or Seattle's Civic Center, Lake Sammamish's southern shore or the Army Depot in Auburn? I can't believe all of this."

I looked over at her, yes she is a school teacher, and she loves to have all the facts, "Thank you for the history lesson, I needed one today. What would I have done without my history lesson? Esther, what in the world does this have to do with me?"

"Everything." She sat down right next to me with the widest eyes I had ever seen on her, and with her broad smile said, "It has everything to do with you, Gracie. Look, this committee is making plans to do something like a World's Fair in Seattle."

"And?"

"And, I think you should look into, IF, and only if, they are going to have sections of the Fair like the one in San Francisco you keep talking about."

"You mean, when I saw Sally Rand and her '*ranch*'?

"It might be a bit ahead of the time they would have everything organized, but it doesn't hurt to contact them and see if they would 'entertain' the idea of having Gracie Hansen's Follies at the World's Fair."

I looked at her and first thought she was completely nuts, but second, thought she was absolutely, "brilliant! Esther, this is exactly what I have been looking for. Do you really think this is something that could happen?"

"You never know until you ask. And I have known you for a very long time, you are not one NOT to ask!" She kissed me on the forehead, and as she headed out the door she turned, "And Gracie, you should be happy you are not married to Leo. You have stepped back a bit, but in that department you are miles ahead without him."

I leaned onto that cot and cried again. Maybe prayers, even for Gracie Hansen, get answered, too.

It was raining hard and I believe that was May. In June school got out and Sambo was around more, or less. He was growing so fast and he had several friends he liked to hang out with more than *liquor store Mom*.

Summer hummed along and soon it was again time for the Loggers' Jubilee. Don't you like how we set our calendar for certain events? The Loggers' Jubilee was one of those calendar events.

Now, I hadn't seen Leo for months, but true to Leo Hansen's nature, there he was with the rest of his logger buddies. So, I tried to stay away the best I could. Then came my birthday – it happens once a year even if I think it shouldn't. As usual it wasn't celebrated, and maybe that was a good thing.

But two days later, just as I was closing the store up that night, guess who shows up waving a piece of paper, singing? Yep, Esther was singing in her best singing voice, which wasn't saying much, dear soul, "Happy Birthday dear Gracie, Happy Birthday to you, Happy Birthday dear Gracie, have I got something great for you. Ta da!" A phone number, "Gracie, this is THE phone number to contact the World's Fair, and I have it neatly written out for my dear friend. Now, I know your birthday was on Saturday, and today is Tuesday, and I know I'm a bit behind, but I couldn't see you until I got this number in my hot little hand." She was shaking it at me, proudly, "here, take it before I explode!"

The numbers were all there.

"Do you want me to leave, or can I stay?"

"Stay, why would you leave?"

"I just thought you wanted to call them privately."

"No, I need someone to give me courage, so stay." I walked over to the phone. "This will be long distance and all."

"CALL!"

And I did, I called. Gracie Hansen called on August 25, 1959 and when I got through I was a bit tongue-tied. But I gave them my address, "PO Box 263, Morton, Washington, and told them I was hoping that they would entertain having a girls show like Sally Rand had in San Francisco at the unnamed Fair coming up." It sounded a bit weird, but I made the first move and it felt good. No, it felt great. Maybe all the work on the Morton Follies and all the ups and downs was preparation for the 'next big thing'.

I turned and looked at Esther. "I did it."

"I know, I heard, but now what?"

"They'll get back with me."

She ran over and hugged me, "It'll all come true, you'll see."

I didn't know how they were going to get hold of me, I had given them my address, but I had forgotten to give them my phone number. Should I call them back and tell them? Does that sound too desperate?

Nope, this time Gracie was going to do something that she doesn't like to do: wait.

Within two weeks I received a letter in the mail.

September 11, 1959

Mrs. Grace Hanson
PO Box 263
Morton, Washington
Dear Mrs. Hanson:

Thank you for your inquiry regarding the Century 21 Exposition. Your name will be placed in our active file so that you will receive our future mailings.

The first information brochure on exhibits and concessions will be completed about the middle of this month. This will be followed by a more detailed brochure containing space costs, regulations, and other information regarding participation.

Pending the availability of more detailed information, I am enclosing a fact sheet which will provide a broad outline of the purposes and plans for the Exposition.

Sincerely,

M. Joanne Dunn, Supervisor
Exhibitor Information

I sat down and re-read the letter and looked over the specifications. 'Well, Gracie, it's not a rejection letter.'

And about the same time another door opened. Tom. But this time instead of parking just in front of the store and going across the street, he got out and walked through my front door.

Tall and handsome as ever, but he looked worried. "Gracie, I want to talk to you, is this an okay time?"

I looked around the store, "if it were busier I'd tell you to come back, but looks like all the customers have found what they were looking for and left. What can I do for you?" I motioned to one of the chairs by the register.

"I'm here to tell you things and afterwards...if there is an afterwards."

"Well, since we haven't really had a beginning, we can't really have anything remotely looking like an afterwards. I just want you to know, whatever is going on seems pretty important, and I'm here to listen."

And I did. Tom was from Morton, like I said. He fell in love with a local Morton girl, Beulah, and before long they moved to Los Angeles where he joined the LAPD. His first assignment was in the traffic division patrolling West Hollywood and Santa Monica Boulevard on a motorcycle, then, working his way up to being on the vice squad. He was there for seven years, and during that time they had two boys, Tom Jr. and Billy. Beulah wanted to move closer to home, so Tom brought the family to West Linn, Oregon, where Maureen was born in 1958.

He started playing with his hands, "While we were in LA she started hearing voices. I was scared for her, and for the boys. She needed help. We went to a doctor and after telling him what had been happening, he said it seemed that she had what he would describe as a mental illness known as manic-depressive disorder – not curable, but treatable. Then we found out that she was pregnant and I knew that if things were to get better, doing what she wanted, getting her closer to home, might make things a bit easier. After Maureen was born, Grace, she wasn't herself. We argued a lot, it wasn't a happy home. And..."

His voice began to quiver but he continued, "now, I just got word that the kids aren't being taken care of properly and the State wants to take them away.'

"She's that bad?"

"Worse than we all had ever thought. You see, I'm gone a lot because of my job and well, I'm going to take the kids up to family in Bellingham and then..." A whisper comes out of his mouth, "Beulah's brother is going to help me take her to the State Mental Hospital near Tacoma once we get things arranged, probably in the late summer, where she'll be committed, probably forever."

I sat there and thought and looked at this man who was holding so much inside, and then I said, "I too have gone through some hell. Bad marriage, and other things, but if you know what you are headed to, you'll make it."

"Gracie, I parked outside to see you every day. I wished I didn't have a trunk full of baggage, but I am truly a good man." He took a deep breath, "I'm lonely and I believe you are also. Can two lonely people find a bit of joy?"

I don't know. I didn't know how to respond. "find a bit of joy?" Where do you find that word in the dictionary anyway? Who made it up? Joy. Oh, right, when I held Sambo in my arms, or at the first night of the first Follies – but now, joy?

I leaned over and kissed him. Again, I don't know why, but I did. It just felt right. Then I pulled back and said, "Tom, I'm my own person now. My son is growing up and I have a life to live. It wasn't my choice to live in Morton, but it is my choice to leave, and I will do that soon. I am not a good mother, housekeeper, but I am a damn good cook. Be kind to me, and I'll return the same. But nothing is going to happen until you get a divorce, it's just not me."

He got up, walked to the door, and then without turning around, "I hope you will wait for me."

"I'm not leaving yet and you know where the front door to my home is."

I had a lot of time on my hands. Sambo liked staying over at the Lesters' and well, someone had to watch the store. I started thinking about the Exhibition and what I wanted to accomplish, and I started thinking about Tom and what he wanted to accomplish. Would either of them work out?

I didn't hear from Tom or the Exhibition until the next spring. During that time, what I did was tell everyone at Christmas my plans, dreams and hopes for the Exhibition. I don't know if George Sr. had anything to do with this, but soon after a letter appeared in my mailbox:

April 11, 1960
Mrs. Grace Hanson, Manager
Washington State Liquor Store
Morton, Washington
Dear Mrs. Hansen:

Joe Alderson, Administrative assistant to the Governor, wrote me that you had some interest in participation of some kind in Century 21.

Would you be so good as to drop me a line and outline in some detail what your thoughts are on the matter. Then, I shall be very pleased to follow through in any way possible.

Sincerely,

Alfred R. Rochester
Executive Director

Century 21 Commission

I couldn't wait. I called him and an appointment was made for Thursday, April 14th at 11:00 am.

It was a school day, so thank goodness Sambo didn't have to do the long drive. I had barely enough gas in the tank but I made it just in time.

I was greeted pretty promptly and shown right in to Mr. Rochester's office. I've always said, I arrived with 'Morton mud on my shoes' (which doll, isn't far from the truth). I told him that I felt that I first had to outline my ideas in person and then with that I would put it down in an official proposal.
He sat there very politely, but I noticed that he was doing a lot with a piece of paper and pen. When I ran out of words he lay down his pen and said, "you know, it's really too soon to make a commitment, it's almost two years away." And as he walked me to the door, he stated again, "A girlie show, you say?"
Quickly I said, "tasteful girlie show."

I think that all the boys at Century 21 were amused at my idea, at least I hoped they were. All the way home I felt like I had blown it, was that good or bad that it was a 'girlie show'? What else would I have called it? But it was two years away and Seattle was a long way away.

I wasn't just working on my 'girlie show', oh no...Gracie had other fish to fry. During this time I was taking courses on hypnosis. And while the Century 21 guys were trying to figure out who I was, I was working on my future, if it wasn't going to be the fair. I believe that there is mind over matter, and on April 26 I received my certificate: *This is to Certify that Gracie Diana Hansen having successfully passed the written examinations pertaining to the science of hypnosis, and proving proficiency in the subject as taught by the Hypnological Research Company of Olympia, Washington, is hereby awarded this certificate of graduation. Denton C Johnson, Director.* I was going to have a future and I was working hard toward it.

No matter how I tried, I couldn't stop thinking about the opportunity that I could be having if only the Century 21 guys would let me do what I wanted. So in August I get anxious and called. It was now a year and a half away and I still didn't have a firm grip on what they would be wanting. Two days later I get this letter;

Mr. Elfron has told me about his discussion with you yesterday and of your telephone call this date. As requested, we are enclosing two additional sets of concessionaire information to aid you in preparing your formal proposal. We appreciate your interest in the Exposition, and look forward to hearing further from you.

Robert D Ashley – Legal Advisor and Acting Director of Concessions.

I have somewhere to start from now, and well, Gracie, you have your work cut out for you. And thank goodness for the 'two additional sets of concessionaire information' – they helped a lot.

What I didn't know, since I wasn't reading the newspapers like Esther was doing every day, was that for many on the Century 21 board, they were determined that the fair "be strictly a high-minded cultural and scientific deal."

By October I hadn't heard from anyone, so I called and told the polite girl on the line that "no matter what, I was still very interested in participating in the Exhibition and please, if you wouldn't mind, keeping my file open?"
The response on the other end was, "Sure."
Was I convinced or should I be worried. It became almost impossible to sit in Morton, knowing phone calls and letters weren't going to open many doors; my face had to be on those doorsteps. I went to Esther and told her what I was feeling. Without hesitation she agreed.
"I know many people are going to think I'm crazy for leaving a Civil Service job, and especially since I won't be vested for retirement or anything, but I have to do this and see if any doors open."
Esther chuckled, "I think you'd better get your tush a-movin', right?"
I hurried back to the store, called George Sr. and told him my plans. He told me that he didn't think it was 'that crazy of an idea', and that he would use what he could within his power and position to help get me a job in Seattle. 'At least if you work at a Savings and Loan, you will be coming with some banking experience, and that is a plus.'

It wasn't long before an interview was set up with Mr. Robert Chinn of United Savings and Loan Associates, a semi-friend of George Sr.'s and one willing to help out a nut job like me. The day of the interview I also lined up places to live. Gracie was on a mission, and if one or the other worked out, at least I was leaving Morton – hopefully forever.

Now during this time, Tom and I dated a bit. Okay, a lot. I shared with him my dream and he told me that he would support me, in fact he would leave his position with Pork and come up to Seattle with me. His kids were still in Bellingham and Sambo was in Morton, but maybe bringing us all together as a unit might make the move easier. Crazy? Well, he was now divorced and so was I, and if everyone thought we were a family it might just make this all come together.

Marriage for us at that moment was out of the question. Why jump from a fire into the frying pan, right? And if anyone asked I would just say, 'I kept Hansen because of my notoriety with the Morton Follies.' And of course once I even dared talk about the Follies, that allowed me to chat about the Exhibition and my ambition.
So we found a house, one big enough for what would eventually be the six of us.

Sambo was in junior high, and it was agreed that he be allowed to stay with the Esthers' in Morton. He was doing so well, and of course, doing well in school was important. Tom Jr., seven, was in the third grade; Bill, six, was in the second, and Maureen (who I started calling Sis about then), was about two and half, not even ready for school. Tom Sr. worked as a bartender to bring in some money, a step down from an undersheriff, but he wanted bringing the family together to work as much as I did.

And I tried my best, but now having four kids in one house with the age range, it was a lot of 'we'll get through this somehow.'

SEATTLE

'You beat something long enough, you're bound to make a dent!'

Mr. Chinn hired me on the spot. I almost dropped dead. He thought bringing in someone like me would liven up the place, plus he said, "your reference from Ross Dill is almost above reproach, he has nothing but praise for you."

So, I stood at the counter, taking deposits and handing out money. All the time I kept thinking, 'I'm one step closer to the front door.'

That Christmas the six of us celebrated as one unit. It was nice having Sambo there, even though I knew in just days he'd be going back to Morton, once school started up again. I brought out the Singer sewing machine and sewed a lot that year. For Sis, I made her a cute little red velvet and white lace trim Christmas dress. I got a petticoat slip to go underneath, but she said every time she wore it, it made her itch. I kept telling her, 'Sis, such are many things in life.' I don't think she understood, but I felt if I said it then, she'd remember when life got a bit rough. I sure enjoyed 'dressing her up.' For Tom I made several jazzy vests and matching ties (I thought this would help with his customers – you know, a point of conversation) but I made sure all three boys got boy stuff.

Christmas dinner was on the table, we all sat down and then I realized, this was more than just for one meal – it was for keeps, and for the first time since Tom and I agreed on this arrangement did I say inside, 'this is all right with me.'

My Christmas present? Well, during the holiday break, I sat down and wrote out my proposal to the Century 21 board. Forcing myself to look through the paperwork, it stated that there would be various buildings that would be called pavilions, and each pavilion would either be permanent or temporary. And that the pavilion and everything about it would be the responsibility of the party leasing the pavilion. My first thought was, what should 'we' call the pavilion.

Sitting alone and knowing that the 'we' was just me, I said, 'well, since it's just you girl, you might as well let everyone know who's responsible and thus the name was born: *Gracie Hansen's Paradise Pavilion*. I already had a company, *Gracie Hansen's Enterprises,* so why not continue the theme. Carl seemed to think the idea was pretty good, and with a few changes and giving his advice the best he could, he made it look official. I signed it on January 16, 1961 and mailed it in.

I hadn't heard if this was still something anyone wanted, but I remember the letter back in April when Mr. Rochester asked in his letter, 'drop me a line and outline in some detail what your thoughts are on the matter.' So, I was dropping him a line all right, an initial proposal to boot!

And here is how life goes. About the same time early 1961 it was reported that State Senator Reuben Knoblauch complained to the World's Fair Commission that there was too much emphasis and space devoted to an art exhibit, so it was agreed to bring in a cadaver to the medical exhibit in the Canadian pavilion to help draw large crowds. AND, that maybe adding some 'skin shows' would do the same thing. Once I heard this, I jumped for joy. It wasn't just me who thought it was a good idea, but now the government of Washington was a bit leery that science and technology wasn't going to attract enough people. So off I went to see if NOW I could get some sort of contract, a deal, anything that would allow me to produce at the World's Fair. I was greeted again with skepticism, but by the time I left it was agreed that if $125,000 was brought to the table, a contract would be given and I could produce my 'girlie show'.

Don't tell me that standing at the front door doesn't help. Off I went back to the Savings and Loan and anyone who walked up to my window that had a high balances and seemed friendly, I wrote down the name, address and phone number.

I also called around to Carl, Pork and others I knew to see if they would like to invest – invest and get their money back if it broke even or made money. No takers. Kind of like, 'don't give Gracie money on something that won't pan out.' Or 'call us later when others invest.'

That was not going to stop me. I worked hard at work, at home, and saw that since I might just be staying in the Savings and Loan industry a bit, I went back to college and, (ready, Mom?) graduated from the Pacific Northwest Savings and Loan School for Executives at the University of Washington. I guess it was just in me or again I was being rewarded for something from the past, but Mr. Chinn promoted me to Assistant Manager. This just opened more doors for me to tell people about my dream.

This time it wasn't just large balances or 'nice people', I was becoming acquainted with many people of Seattle who had real money. And I began checking them off.

I would go and call on them on my lunch, or after work, or on Saturdays, and I would give them this pitch: "Have you ever been to a World's Fair, or know anyone who has? And, if so, what do you remember? 'Cause you know what they *all* remember: Little Egypt, Sally Rand, Billie Rose and some of those things. And *no one* can tell you about an exhibit they saw any place! So I formulated my pet theory: Science will *never* replace sex or cotton candy." But nothing was working. And after spending the lunch with my last possible prospect, I walked in and told Mr. Chinn that I was "at the end of the list."
He looked up at me and said, "Gracie, I've been watching you for months. You have not only gone to college, graduated, advanced into an Assistant Manager, but you are still trying to make this 'girlie show' idea work. How much are you trying to raise?"
When I told him $125,000, I thought he'd say, "well, good luck, now let's get back to work." But no, he said, "okay then, let's see what friends can do for us."

And, believe you me, it wasn't more than an hour and a half later that he walked into my office and said, "will $90,000 do?"

"What did you do, rob your own bank?"
He sat down and said, "I called twenty-eight of my friends and relatives and eighteen of them agreed to put up $5,000 each."
Without thinking I said, "I need to convert to being Chinese!"
He laughed and said that legal documents would have to be gathered and signed. I told him that since my brother was an attorney, maybe he'd at least start the process. With that, he looked at me, "what is the amount you need right now?"
Well, to be honest, anything over a dollar is what I needed, but I told him that I would have to check with the Century 21 board.
As he left he stopped and said, "good luck to all of us."

All that was needed to do the initial paperwork was $500 and Mr. Chinn was more than happy to draw the check and have it sent to the Century 21 Exhibition on March 23rd. I now was officially on target to open the *Gracie Hansen's Paradise Pavilion*.

With Mr. Chinn's help, Mr. Clay Nixon became my lawyer and, with Carl's help, drew up the Articles of Incorporation, *"Paradise International: 625 Jackson Street, Seattle WA – Gracie Hansen,"* and they were signed on March 28.

What I didn't know for months is that Mr. Chinn's wife was a huge supporter of the arts in Seattle. Did she persuade or was it Gracie's charm? Either way, I felt I was on my way.

Then I hit a wall. I was working so hard at moving forward on Paradise Pavilion and at the Savings and Loan, it seemed like nothing was getting done at home. I couldn't quit the Savings and Loan until the Fair started and everything fell into place so, swallowing what pride I had, it was decided that we needed a housekeeper.

But even with her help, I, personally, couldn't do both jobs for much longer, so I sat down and talked to Mr. Chinn. Again it was like he knew just what I was going to say. His comment to me was, "When things start feeling like the investment is being compromised by you working here, it's best that you leave and focus on making that money grow."

On May 2nd talks started on a space agreement. When the Pavilion was originally discussed it was going to be a venue on the *Boulevards of the World* area of the park. But it was soon discovered that it might be best if it be relocated to the end of the Fair, closer to the north stadium stands. It seemed more logical for me, because this would mean that those who only wanted to come to my pavilion didn't have to go through the Fair's turnstiles and pay the additional expense. But, when I heard the area was going to be called Sin Alley, I raised some questions. "When is sex a sin? If it is, then we all are doing a great deal of it."

Within two days a space rental agreement was worked out. And I pulled together a team to help me design a quality proposal, and, boy, was it ever. I didn't have a clear sense of who was going to choreograph the show. I had heard about Jack Card from British Columbia, who had gained some prominence in the theatrical field. He agreed to be named as the choreographer. Did we have a contract? No. Should we have? Yes. I put his name in the proposal anyway, but I couldn't get a firm commitment from him. He either wouldn't return calls or he would say, "it's just too far away, we'll talk later." Later never happened and putting his name in the final proposal 'looked good,' but watch what you put in print. I'll get to that later.

Being the frustrated ham that I am, I been reading *Variety* and the show business papers for a while, and I knew that there were two big names in the business who did first-class shows: Don Arden and Barry Ashton. I took some time off work around June or July and made a trip to Las Vegas and Los Angeles. I talked to Don Arden and Barry Ashton. If I couldn't have Jack Card, then either one of these guys would be even better.

When I got hold of Don he listened intently and liked the whole concept; however he was committed to producing the famous

Lido Shows in Paris and at the Stardust in Vegas. So, I went with little expectation about getting a yes from Barry. He too liked the idea of being the choreographer, but it might have to be more – was that okay? I didn't have anything, so 'a little more – sure.'

He told me confidentially that he was going to be signing a contract to have the exclusive rights to the Ziegfeld Follies – Mrs. Ziegfeld was meeting with him in the next day or so. Without thinking twice, I agreed to bring him on board as choreographer and would he consider being producer of the show as well? He agreed only if Lloyd Lambert could design costumes. I needed first class, and it seemed like that was what I was getting.

While in Las Vegas, agreements had been worked out that both Barry and Lloyd would be traveling up to Seattle in mid to late October, and I would arrange some photos, press releases and start getting word out.
Barry said, "You've got to let people know what you are up to early, it gets their tongues to wag, and then when you hit with press and ads, tickets start to sell. It happens all the time here in Las Vegas."
So off I went back to Seattle and hired a PR firm. To be honest, I didn't even know press agents existed until Barry told me about them!

The two press agents were great - Guy Williams and Bob Karolevitz. Before I knew it they had put me in outfits designed by John Eaton, a local designer of some renown, and more ostrich feathers and baubles than you could count. They helped me with my speech and helped me find my footing, okay, my way of saying little one-liners, but to be honest, I was pretty good at those already.

I now had 'the look' – oh, I had a look, thanks to Guy, Bob and

John Eaton. I guess I had always had 'A look' but Gracie Hansen now had '<u>the</u> look' and I tell you – I almost didn't know who she was staring back in the mirror. I had big hair, big lips, big jewelry – I wasn't just big in the hips anymore, I was big all over. And I loved it!

The final proposal given to the Century 21 organization had on the front a woman – sideways with long flowing hair. That didn't quite say what I wanted it to say. What I wanted was there to be something that when you saw it, you knew Gracie Hansen was behind it.

I told Guy and Bob, and they immediately called in Bob Todd, who was a local graphic artist. He kept asking me questions and drawing things on a pad. When I told him I wanted the show to be a little naughty and a little nice, he smiled. When I told him that I loved the idea that like an apple you have to take a bite out of life to know if you really like it or not, 'I wish we could use that, an apple with a bite out of it.' Right then, he lifted his pad and there it was – what I had been searching for, a delicious apple with a bite out of one side. And I have used that ever since. It says so much, without saying anything at all.

And soon, I was no longer on the payroll of the United Savings and Loan but working full-time for Gracie Hansen's Enterprises.

Barry and Lloyd arrived with possible sketches in hand and a photo session was arranged. On November 3rd the Seattle Times published a photo of the three of us reviewing what they say are the 'blueprints' for a World's Fair Theater-Cafe.

Barry was right, the phone started ringing. I started feeling a bit uneasy – I was now on payroll working for Gracie Hansen's

Paradise, so were Guy, Bob, Barry and Lloyd.....what I didn't have was a signed contract from Century 21.

I was also feeling uneasy about how I was treated, with just 'a girlie show'. But, I think bringing in a wad of cash, it won't be about memos here or a piece a paper there...it will be a serious statement and a contract.

So I went to Mr. Chinn and asked if there was a way I could take in all $90,000 in cold hard cash. He looked up at me and through his glasses I saw a worried look on his face. "Look, you can trust me, I am not going to run away with it. I want a contract with the Century 21, and I think the only way they are going to give it to me is by me producing as much money as I can. They've been pretty cold to me this far, and I think this will 'warm them up'." That afternoon, I left with my purse full of many denominations but in it was the $90,000. I went to the Century 21 offices and there was a meeting going on. What timing, right? When I arrived they couldn't or didn't want to be disturbed. I told the lady at the desk, "for this, they'll want to be disturbed." And I lay the purse on the edge of the desk and opened it up.

She looked up at me, quickly went into the conference room. It wasn't even a minute, she was out, and I was greeted to come in and talk to the group. That's all I needed, an invitation. "Look, boys, you said that I had to bring at least $125,000 to you before any contract negotiations could truly begin. Well, a couple weeks ago, a $500 check was sent to secure our deposit and here," slowly opening my purse, "is another $90,000 in cold, hard cash as an advance guarantee against receipts."

Oh, and I received the contract right then and there, after I turned over the cash and it was counted.

Now, what I didn't know, and there are times that you shouldn't know everything, right? It seems that while I was getting my ducks in a row, so were the men of Century 21. You see, that was on the 16th of November, but what I didn't know was that on November 15th, George K. Whitney (Director of Concessions and Amusements for Century 21) sent a letter to San Francisco's Hotsy Totsy Club. In his letter he stated that he would like someone to bring in a "theater-restaurant night club similar in scope and program" to that city's Bimbo's 365 Club (which incidentally Barry Ashton had staged). The letter went on to say that a prime space was available, that Barry Ashton had been hired, and with everything in place, this "would be the hit of Show Street." There was one caveat, since the Grand Opening was being held on April 21st, they needed to take immediate action.

Thank goodness for my gut feelings about going there on the 15th, right? And, he wasn't lying either, Barry Ashton was hired, but not by them.

Soon after, Century 21 agreed that 'Show Street', as it was to be called, would be in Building 90 located at the corner of Fifth Avenue and Mercer Street. When I talked to Fair officials it was always, "Yeah, over there in Building 90." Like that was the back forty on a farm! Anyway, the design was a U-shaped complex of buildings for "Adults Only" attractions. There would be, of course, *Gracie Hansen's Paradise Pavilion*, then the *Polynesian Playhouse* (I don't know how adult that got), the *Diamond Horseshoe* (with a Gay Nineties theme), *The Galaxy* (and its *Girls of the Galaxy* show), *The Le Petit Theatre* (an adult puppet show), and *Backstage U.S.A.* (hosting a risqué "Peep" show). There seemed to be a lot of attraction being added to this U-shaped complex, when not too long ago, it was me, alone, fighting get my show approved – now there six 'adult-themed' attractions? Thank goodness mine featured a dinner and a show!

December 21, 1961, is a big day for me.

First, my name made it into Time Magazine. You can hear me giggling now, can't you? What was it, two years ago I was in Morton looking at water falling down the back of the liquor store wall? The article stated that, yes, worry not, "the fair will have its undraped girls, in a 'Las Vegas-type revue' to be produced by one Gracie Hansen, an entrepreneur' who promises 'a daring show with some nudity, but all in good taste.'" And it would take place on Show Street - the titillation zone of the fair located at the northeast corner of the grounds.

Second, I was about to do something I had dreamed of for what seemed like forever – me, standing on a little platform with a back wall on the construction site of *Gracie Hansen's Paradise Pavilion*, wearing my mom's mink stole, white gloves and a wonderful white hat with feathers.

I walked up to the podium and said, "This is my dream come true. I'm just a country girl from Morton. Very naive. Why, I didn't know there were press agents until a few months ago." Then I was handed a 'gold-plated' shovel, and in the floor of the platform was a hole, "I'm digging for diamonds. Diamonds are a girl's best friend - but I'll never knock rubies, emeralds or pearls either."

I looked out and there was a sea of people, watching, clapping and laughing with me. "We may go broke, but we'll never be flat busted, and I just want you all to know that I am out to save this Fair from science. There's just too much of it around us – the monorail, the space needle. I tell you right now, science will never replace sex and cotton candy. This show will be a Las Vegas-type show, a daring show with some nudity, but, all in good taste."

Then a newsperson asked about the apple.

"The apple tree in Paradise will be our symbol, and like life, you have to take a bite out of it to see what it's made out of. And for all you 'boys' out there, it is true that some of our showgirls are nude from the waist up. It's not thrust upon you. In fact, sometimes you have to look for them in there. And, as yet, no one has objected and found it distasteful, so I guess it's a matter of presentation." Then I lifted my arm up in the air, as arranged, and one of our girls stepped through the large apple that was painted on the wall. She stood there displaying one of the many costumes the show would have. More applause, laughter and some cheers. Gracie, you are doing the right thing.

Once I grabbed the attention of the press, I knew I couldn't let them out of my sight. God bless press agents, you pay them for a job that you cannot do, or you hire them so they put in jobs that you probably wouldn't do. I got booked to speak and appear anywhere and everywhere; dressed up in a Santa suit to entertain at the Children's Orthopedic Hospital, drive the car around with the top down and yell out 'come see me at the Paradise' or use the diploma I got from Dale Carnegie and do some inspirational talks to booster clubs- I was up for anything. 'Gracie was your gal to get the word out' – it wasn't just the Space Needle that was going to turn around 360 degrees and show you everything!

Lloyd Lambert was busy working on costumes. I began feeling like I should look over the invoices and that's when I noticed that there were going to be a lot of feathers and a lot of money spent on all the feathers. Now, I love feathers, I should have been born a bird, but the total spent on just ostrich feathers was $8,000 I had to see these costumes. Row after row of beautiful, handmade costumes – head dresses, body suits, tuxedos, rhinestone-covered dresses. I turned to Lloyd and said, "I needed to see for myself how beautiful we were all going to look." I thought to myself, "We'll look beautiful, but boy, we'd better not sweat. The cleaning bill alone is going to have Mr. Chinn going through the roof!" What I didn't know until everything was said and done, the costumes for the show would cost $46,000 almost half the $90,000. All I could think is, 'we'd better sell and sell well.'

In just a short four months, after a lot of sweat, sleepless nights and work by Howard Doug, who designed the building, and Strand Company, who were the builders, the building started taking shape. The original designs just had the word Paradise in large letters over the door as you entered and that, to me, didn't sound too welcoming. So I had a big neon sign made that read, *Gracie Hansen's Paradise Pavilion,* and of course with a large apple and the bite out of it.

It did get everyone's attention when it was installed. All lit up in neon, you couldn't miss it from Fifth and Mercer. However, I had not taken into consideration one person's feelings – Mr. Ashton's, Barry.

Everyone came out to see it get lit up and all applauded except one – Barry. He had gone back inside and was on the phone. Now, the way I knew about this was a letter I received from HIS own public relations person. Here goes, we shared Guy and Bob, but after the sign went up, we didn't. It seemed that Barry felt I was trying to 'monopolize the credit for the show's artistic excellence'. I wasn't, I was just zealous – and it cost me dearly. His scorn was worse than any woman's, let me tell you. Oh, and our backers were no longer eighteen Chinese businessmen; it had grown to 40! And when there is a feud, everyone knows about it. I have to tell you, "Don't ever get caught in a feud involving shrewd Oriental businessmen and mean chorus boys."

Tension around "Paradise" was horrible. My paradise was now my hell.

Slowly and diplomatically we made amends. He realized that I was the boss and calling the shots and he was 'just the hired help'. Now I never thought of him that way, but as Toru Sakahara, who was one of the attorneys working for us, explained in a very nice way – "you didn't seek Gracie out, she sought you. She brought you a contract, and you signed it." And, the sign was changed to read: 'Paradise International' in large letters with 'Gracie Hansen presents Barry Ashton's Night in Paradise'. Some more money was spent, which we didn't have, but it repaired a lot of hurt feelings.

When Barry and I did talk again I made sure that he was in charge of his side of the business, the 'onstage side'. It's odd, because he was the one now talking about making some 'minor' changes in the show and what I would be doing for the show. I suggested that I greet people at the door, like a maître'd, laugh at their jokes, give a hug and kiss when needed, and be the good hostess who was throwing a great party. Barry thought I should be on stage. Now, honestly, that is where I wanted to be, but after our tiff with the sign, I didn't want him to feel like I was stepping on his 'artistic' sensibilities.

"Look, we have this great band leader who could rouse the crowd up and then you could walk out and greet the folks, tell a few jokes and if you wanted, sing a song.'"

It was true, Barry and I agreed that hiring John R. Souders (affectionately known as Jackie) to be the band leader for our pit band was a stroke of genius. He was huge in the 20's and everyone would love to see this aged man having a great time each night. I worried that he might be a bit old to play every show, every night, but once Jackie signed on, there was no stopping him.
Barry leaned over, "you know we've kicked around you doing this, and I have always said you remind me of a mix between Mae West, Sophie Tucker and Texas Guinan."

I immediately belted out, "Hi-ya suckers!"
And Barry jumped up and hugged me, "YES!"

The ice that had been part of our lives for the past couple weeks seemed to have melted — over me saying, 'Hi-ya suckers?' If that was the case, I'd say it ten times a day just to keep him happy and, as they say, keep peace in the family.

"You know, I read, I think in Variety, she was the first real female emcee. God, I love her story; someone has to do it someday. She served liquor during prohibition, and it is said that in 1926 alone she made $700,000! If saying 'Hi ya suckers,' telling a joke or two to make that kind of money, I'm your gal."

And that's when the work increased. Not only was I producing the show, chasing money, now I was on stage praying I didn't embarrass anyone. We tried to have me right after the band played the intro and then at the closing of the set. For awhile it seemed like it didn't matter; but we found out during the six months, people actually like me at the end, like saying 'Hi ya, suckers' (and I changed it to 'Hello, suckers') made them feel like, 'look you fools, I got your money, I hope you enjoyed yourselves.'

We were still missing something for the show. Barry didn't want it to be a vaudeville show, but it had a bent toward it, so a suggestion was made that variety acts should be found to round out the singing, dancing, parading and me.

I had a brilliant idea, but I said it slowly just in case Barry felt I was being overbearing. Let's see if the novelty acts from the Ed Sullivan Show would be able to be booked after they appeared on his Sunday broadcast. Barry loved the idea and so did the Ed Sullivan show; they accepted. Every so often we'd get a report of this 'must-see act' and soon they were incorporated on stage.

The two acts that endeared me, Barry, the cast and the whole audience was Dick Weston and 'Aunt Martha', and Bob Williams with his dog, Louie. Bob was an owner-trainer and well, Louie was a show all by himself. He looked like a mutt, really, a real sweet mutt; long ears, short legs, big, soulful eyes. Bob had trained Louie to do commands – in reverse. "Up and at'em, Louie, ole boy, you're a bundle of energy tonight!" And the audience expected Louie to do the command, but Louie, flopped right on the stage acting tired. It kept on going. We couldn't wait for an audience – if my telling jokes, or the girls breasts wouldn't wow them, then we knew by sometime in the evening they would at least love Bob and Louie.

About that time, Guy thought it be a good idea to see if I could get a car dealership to sponsor me and/or the show. So through some connections I met Wayne Hurling of Hurling Brothers Automotives in West Seattle. They had a Buick dealership. Well, we got along so well, that he let me use a brand new 1962 Buick Electra 225 convertible. I asked if it was okay if I could modify it just a bit. He looked at me and said, "how so?"
"Well, if I could have the door handles 'gold' plated and my apple painted on doors, that would do me just fine." To be honest, I do not think he knew what he was getting himself into, but in no time, that Buick was sitting in the driveway, the kids were impressed, Tom couldn't believe his eyes and Gracie had another way to advertise the Paradise Pavilion.

Now that I was getting press it seemed more and more that I was being looked at as some 'evil woman' or a 'woman without morals' by some, but the press kept on writing about me and my "Paradise" with topless women and a logo that had an apple with a bite out it. Sure sounded a lot racier than it was, but after dealing with the Morton Methodists, I knew that most were thinking that I was Satan and had the apple that Adam ate when Eve tempted him with it.

And with the press and the 'evil' I was spreading, my endeavor was definitely on the Seattle Censor Board's radar, as well as the other shows in 'Building 90'. It took some doing, but they were persuaded to look beyond just the bare-breasted women and look at the potential of what the Show Street/ Entertainment Street would present. I kept telling the press and anyone who would listen to me, "it's going to be a little naughty and nice." Their approval came only days before the fair was to open. The press had a field day, especially with the headline:

'Censors OK Fair Nudies.'

The 'bosom barrier' was broken this weekend as Seattle censors passed the last of the shows on Show Street which will glorify the female form at Seattle's World's Fair for the first time in the straitlaced Northwest. Gracie Hansen's lavish Las Vegas-type revue was the first to satisfy the censors. There was never any question about the Hawaiian Village, which is pure Polynesian. The galaxy of girls, a slow tableau of undraped figures, also passed the acid test, to the surprise of even the most blasé previewers. Portlander Jack Matlack's Hollywood models undressing, "showering", dressing and parading in 'Peep Backstage' were prudish by comparison. The 25 selected lovelies all wore some covering and performed behind a defusing scrim or gauze curtain, as presumably required by the censors. If the show down the street can keep abreast of the times, why can't I? Leroy Prinz, producer of the show, was heard to say to the censors. Final round of this battle of the bosoms will be fought out in a new viewing when Prinz' girls will perform without so much covering.

I don't know if it was the press that was pressuring or someone or something higher up, but all of us working on the pavilion kept saying, 'it's all going to come together or it will all fall apart.' We weren't the only ones sweating bullets, Syd and Marty Krofft from Los Angeles brought up an adult-only puppet show called 'Les Poupées de Paris'. Les Poupées, was a French puppet farce but with overt risqué sexual overtones and had to be hastily rewritten to suit local standards of propriety and just made it under the wire to open on April 21st. They weren't competition to us, officially, but anything that caused a show on Show Street to be cancelled was bad press and bad business for us all. But, as with everything, there was one show that did close the very day after the Fair opened. It was called the 'Girls of the Galaxy', where young women posed naked for visitors with cameras. Even my girls didn't do that!

And the other problem was the Blue Law – the no liquor sold on Sunday law. No joke. The State Liquor Control Board had decreed no alcohol would or could be served on Sunday. And that finally it was agreed that, yes, Sundays at the fair would be dry as well, no exception. It was so ridiculous when even the French Pavilion had to display only empty bottles of wine, lest anyone be tempted and steal them. And then I heard that this right-wing old fart named Westbrook Pegler was saying, "You've got to have booze on Sunday…you can't run a World's Fair like a Methodist camp meeting." I couldn't agree more, but through all the battles in the press, one thing stood fast and true, the Blue Law was not to be changed 'just because of the fair.' And it stayed that way until 1967.

It's been reported, and it's true, that before the Pavilion opened, close to a half-million dollars had been spent and yes, because I was trying out my new life as a woman of Chinese descent, almost all of our staff were Chinese. Another great investment. And, I also want to let you know, I wasn't going to open the Pavilion, no matter who was who – there had to be a plaque on the outside entrance that read, 'This would not be possible without Esther.'

Night before opening...I would tell you how I felt, but here is what the press thought about our 'preview.'

April 20, 1962 Grace's Show Nice, Not Naughty
By ELMER OLSON
Managing Editor The Daily Chronicle

CENTURY 21 — "I dreamed of it back in Morton," she said. Maybe, but we doubt it. That's what Gracie Hansen, who says she's "only a country girl, "told nearly 700 newspaper, radio and television people here Thurs- Paradise International theatre restaurant will be the brightest, most colorful spot on Show Street of the 1962 Seattle World's Fair. Wait and see. It'll have to live down some of its advance publicity — a lot of it from Gracie. Grace's pitch that the show is "nudie but nice" doesn't hit the mark. But that some bareness, can still keep day night in a preview of a There is "Night in Paradise." Las Vegas Like it or not, depending on distinction, your interests and tastes, Grade's A Gracie's place on Show Street

Features more first class entertainment than it does bare girls, has sound, color and style, and most of it is in good taste. While huge neon tubing over Gracie's Paradise depicts sin as a huge apple, with a bite taken out of it, the place is no bump and grind tent show. The inside is all modern design and tastefully done, if loud. And if it's a night club, it's the plushiest in the northwest. There's a half - circle stage and a burlesque runway. The runway is little more than a design feature. It's not used much and it's not needed. There are girls, girls, girls. But no strippers, and only a few high kicks. The form divine is shown in a space-age packet. Ballet is used, coupled with vivid color and action. The costumes win plaudits, not necessarily for scantiness, but for color and design. While the girls, girls, girls aren't on, the stage is held *down by some half - dozen acts, from acrobatics to unicycle riders. They're all top-quality acts. Gracie — all of her in a floor length white gown with a toga thrown over her left shoulder — greeted all the guests at the door. She had seven-inch crystal eardrops against her cold black hair. She had a huge crystal bracelet on her left arm. She walked in a "crop spray" of heady perfume. On the stage after the show, she said, "bless you all" and reminded her audience she was "just a homely country girl." She added the girls, girls, girls have 736 performances to drudge through yet. If you want to see "Paradise" the cover charge is $3 a head. You can buy liquor and food, and you can say "hi" to Gracie.*

Then opening day, what a day it was. I have to laugh, and you do at such things, but it was almost chaos. There were 'gates' you had to go through which were supposed to open at 11 am. Well, someone had lost the West Gate key, and it opened about twenty-two minutes late.

There all these big honcho's for the opening ceremonies at the Memorial Stadium and then there was this 'electronic countdown machine,' they called it. I guess it was started two years before by then-President Eisenhower. The machine was designed to count down the days, hours, minutes, and seconds toward zero when the Fair was officially to open. And, almost on cue, the clock struck zero and John Raitt sang 'Meet Me at the Needle.' A twenty-one-gun salute proceeded his singing and the next thing I knew, I heard bells ringing and balloons were released in the air. It kept going on and on...and before you knew it, the dew cleared and the sun finally broke through and wow...it was like that too was planned. What got my heart really racing was when I heard that Elvis Presley was going to be coming, not only to be 'at the fair' but to do a movie at the Fair!

Heading back to the pavilion I was struck how weird to have the kids amusement right close to our complex; it cost nearly

$2,000,000 and they called it 'The GayWay', just like the San Francisco World's Fair. I don't know how many families were gay or happy about having their children be so close to 'sin'.

And then, our opening night. I couldn't sit still. We were booked out for several months (thank goodness, there were bills to pay and investors to worry about) but that didn't mean we could just sit back. By then Barry had cooled his heels about me trying to sabotage his creation; I think he understood, it was my creation and inspiration, and with his talent WE pulled it off. Today he seemed pleased with everything, smiling, hugging and giving pointers here and asking for some of us to do sections of the show 'just one more time – just in case'. This must be the way it feels when a show on Broadway was opening – well, Seattle and the world, I was opening my big Broadway show and it was guaranteed to run for at least six months – here we come! It was a fantastic opening night, too – the governor was there – the whole Seattle City Council – it was the Who's Who of Seattle.

After the shows that night, Guy came up to me and said, 'Seattle is a wonderful city. The whole town is slavering to get in and see the bare breasts, but they all came out talking about a trained dog.'

During the fair I was asked to speak to twenty five Lutheran ministers meeting at Menucha. I told them flat out, "Your business and mine are just the same, except mine, is better. You and I offer entertainment, music, and we both pass the hat. But my people all leave smiling and happy." I've always said, religion should be happy. "You have to put more show-manship in it. And change the hours." Then I invited them to see the show. I got the loveliest thank you letters from them. I then sent them to Mom. She never did tell me if she received them or not.

Where was the 'family' during all of this? I feel a bit guilty about this. Here they all were, thrown into a house and, without saying a word, had to find a way to get along and not have me around. I have to think that many times they just stood there and shook their heads. To be honest, it wasn't talked about much. The boys were involved with school, Maureen was just heading off to school and, well, Tom, god bless him, was still working as a bartender. To 'reward' him during my free time, (you ask when? I'll respond rarely) I made eighty to ninety vests that sparkled and dazzled and, may have been over the top, but I wanted Tom to know that these were "products of love from Gracie" and without him none of what I was doing would mean a lot. Here I had a man who, no matter what, did not, ever, complain. Maybe I could be like Mom with regard to relationships. First, Dad who was an alcoholic and then George who was almost a saint. And me? Leo was an alcoholic and Tom, to me, was a saint. He put up with me. Anybody who puts up with my wigs, eyelashes, boas and the works, IS a saint in my book!

Now, I don't like rumors, and this one bothered me. I was told to me that Doctor Athelston Spilhaus, 'Commissioner' of the Federal Science Pavilion, said, "I'll put my show up against Gracie Hansen's any day."

So, guess what I did? On Monday I went over and 'visited' his show and then noticed I was being followed by a couple people from the press.

One asked, "Gracie you're all dressed up with a mink stole and a flowing hat —why?"

I didn't stop. "Come on boys, I have wanted to see the show for a long time." So we waited in line, just like everyone else. I had to admit there was a pretty good crowd waiting to get in. When we got inside, I discovered that I had to sit on the floor, so down harem-style I went. What to say next? I felt the carpet and liked it, then out came, "Dr. Spilhaus has better carpets." The lights went dim, a movie showed and then we were taken to another room. That's when I met Dr. Spilhaus; tall man, glasses and a suit. After all, he was a Doctor – a doctor of what I wasn't sure, though.

The first words out of his mouth made me a bit mad, "Hi, did you come to see a good show?"

I could not tell the press that I was wanting to get the hell out of there, "I think it's terrific; but it will never replace sex and cotton candy."

He came right back, "I quite agree. Now I want to see your show."

Oh, he's sly, "Won't you be my guest?" Two can play this type of ping pong.

He turned and said, "would you sign our VIP register? Your name will be right under the Empress of Iran."

That did impress me, "The pavilion is beautiful. I enjoyed it so much, I might even make you head angel in Paradise."

He nicely said, "I'd be miscast."

Guy taught me, 'You know when the interview is done so don't prolong it.' I finished writing my name and shook his hand, "Do see our show anyway."

The next day it was in the paper, there I was sprawled out on the nice doctor's carpet – but it was press. And we were getting a lot of press, so much that I was asked to go down to Portland and participate as the Grand Marshall in the Merrykhana Parade –it was the parade the Saturday night before the big Rose Festival Parade; sort of a mardi gras-type parade that featured such things as the 'Rainmakers' who shot water from umbrellas.

It was going to be tricky, but for one night, and the exposure, I believed it was well worth the work. Then, as if it never happened, they withdrew their offer! What the Rose Festival spokesman told the press was, "there was some confusion concerning the role of Mrs. Hansen, as well as a deluge of public protests, they had to withdraw the entry. (Anyway), she and her troupe were to be one of the 100 entries and that they were never to play an official role in the night's event."

Now, just tell me one thing, how can you not be serving in an official role if you were to be the Grand Marshall? No wonder I never considered crossing the Columbia River.

What I loved, though, was the additional mileage I got out of this. Mrs. Weckworth (who I didn't know) wrote a letter to the Oregonian newspaper.

To the Editor: Portland has my sympathy. You must be ashamed of W. R. Moore and the 'women's groups' that influenced his decision to cancel out Gracie Hansen's appearance at the Rose Festival. We in Seattle are very proud of Gracie Hansen, and the very beautiful show she is presenting at her Paradise. She will be one of the three judges who will select a queen for our Wallingford District, to present us in our All-City Sea Fair participation. We feel very fortunate indeed that a woman as busy and as important as she is has been willing to take time to assist us in this fashion.'

Soon after, there was a rumor that I wanted *to be asked and then not asked to be the Grand Marshall "ette" for press reasons. It was stated that "The suspicion grows that this is what Mrs. Hansen wanted. She parlayed her snub into a much ballyhoo bonanza that she could have achieved merely by appearing...she has succeeded in portraying Portland as a blue nosed. Victorian contrasted with sophisticated, modern Seattle."*

I threw up my hands. I <u>wanted</u> to go. At this time we needed the exposure. I have learned you can get all the press you want, but to get the people <u>in</u> the door, you need them to see the goods <u>behind</u> the door.

I think some of this was brought on when I was quoted as saying, *"Gracie Hansen regards Portland's snub...as the next best thing to a police raid of her World's Fair girl show....while she thinks her rejection...was rude...Gracie knows a box office bonanza when she sees one. 'I thought it was terrific...I'd been praying for a raid, you know, now all those nice Portland people will want to come up to Seattle to see the wicked lady."*

Fortunately, this press guy got things right. He even quoted the invitation! *"The entire committee feels it would be an adjunct to our parade if you could find the time from your busy schedule to visit with us in Portland and be part of the fun and frolic on the opening of the Rose Festival."*

Well, I was ready to frolic. "I was going to take three girls from my daytime fashion show down in black cocktail dresses and white fox furs." And I added, "I'm sure they'd be more dressed than some of the majorettes in the parade, who are pretty bare." With everything that was said and done, the one true thing that came out of it? I felt like my old self again.

As you can see, I was getting press. Good **and** bad. As Guy told me, 'press, Gracie is great. It means you are somebody – somebody worth being talked about and others that want to know about.' But I need to tell you something now. You can plan on everything that you can think of, but there is always, always one more way to have the left shoe drop. I didn't anticipate that people didn't want to come and see our show. But it happened.

This headline showed up at the wrong time, in the middle of the run, in the middle of summer, it read, *"Gracie Hansen says, 'That's Show Biz'"*. Now, that headline doesn't make you run to read the story, but when it's on the business page of the newspaper, who reads it? Businessmen, those I needed to come see the show. It was the caption just above the headline that I think did me in, 'Making the dollar.'

I have always been told to be honest 'enough'. But, maybe I was being more than honest when I sat down and chatted with this reporter. It wasn't until I read the article that I began to cry. Not only had he spelled out how terrible he was treated from the front door to his seat, but he also mentioned how small the size of the house was and it just kept going on. Here, let me let you read a little...this is one of the worst reviews I think I have ever gotten – from anyone. I know it wasn't meant or directed at me, but my name was above the door for better or worse. Here goes, *"In Paradise the Oriental waiters who own part of the place smile nervously and walk too fast to show you a table and the guy who does the dog act laughs loud to help the empty seats understand that it is a funny act."* Should I go on? Already you can see – this doesn't sound, look or read like 'hey come on up to Seattle, we're smokin' up here!' Anyway, *"Or as they say at the Century 21 Fair, "They are dying on Show Street."* Now, this is how I felt when I saw 'Queen for a Day' pull up his dress and show the city of Morton his wares. Had I not worked all these years, and for what? I'm sorry, it, um, goes on, *"Well, it isn't so good as it was," admitted Gracie Hansen as she stepped solidly from stages still hungry for breath from the wind-up routine she does on stage."* (Can you tell me what he meant by, 'stepped solidly?') I know my size isn't considered exactly Marilyn Monroe, I'm more Jane Russell...it doesn't end there. *"Grace was wearing black and a big ostrich feather in her hair and several pounds of rhinestones and some eye makeup. But she looked nice anyway* (tell me what he meant by that, that those who wear rhinestones, eye makeup and ostrich feathers in their hair don't look nice? Okay, he was a business reporter not an entertainment reporter...but he was there for an entertainment show) *and when she said to the 30 or so people* (I know, it was miserable, as the theatre holds 700) *of the first show of the afternoon, "This is the adult education center of the Fair Grounds," you couldn't help wishing someone would laugh. "Fun is like insurance,' she told the Iowa-looking audience that had put out $4.00 a piece to get inside, "like insurance, the older you get, the more it costs." Then more of an appeal than a gag line, Grace added, "Every Adam needs his apple-jack." So she laughed herself and the whole thing had left her a little breathless by the time she sat down to talk about the $1.3 million gross business and hopes to do in the 700-capacity house at the end of Show Street where they are dying."* It goes on, but what I tried not to do was run home and crawl under the covers.

It was an interview where no matter what was said, it was going to end up as 'Gracie, you screwed up.' I don't believe anything was screwed up, I just think that if the Pavilion was running between October and May instead the opposite, we'd have been sold out for the run. I knew that the 43 people in the cast, crew and band didn't want to play for only 30 'Iowans' but a union contract, and they were all getting paid union scale, was a union contract and work was work, no matter how many people sat in the house. Kept looking at the ledger and said, 'okay, Gracie, where is the $21,000 coming from for this week's bills?'

It has to turn around, but even though by the end of the Fair almost 10 million people came through the gates, and we got a percentage of them, we struggled, smiled and worked our tails off to entertain those who came. And as I said, it was hard to be on stage looking out and not having anyone in the house, but, harder to go back to the office and see there was no money in the bank to pay the bills. I had heard it said once, 'it's not how you start, it's how you finish.' That's a nice quote, but what do you do during the meantime?

And then another shoe dropped. What now? Do you remember I told you that I had put Jack Card in the final proposal as the choreographer? Well, when he read the press and saw that we were a hit (he should have been at some of the shows during this time), he sent a letter alleging character defamation to me and my company, asking for either a settlement or he would sue. I took it straight to Carl and he agreed that "it could be fought." However, "since Jack Card's name was used to secure partial rights to producing the Paradise Pavilion and since he was never consulted after thorough negotiations, he may have a case."

I tried to argue that he wasn't responsive and that I had to get the staff in place so everything would open on time. But I knew Carl, I knew my brother, and I knew he had my best interests at heart. "You are dealing with artists who have big egos. You bruised an ego here and sis, I'm afraid you are going to have to pay." And pay I did, to the tune of $27,000. A little over one week's needed income. Again I learned a lesson, 'always have a contract in hand – then if they sue, it's in writing.'

I needed some good news – I needed a reason to say, 'you are doing the right thing here, Gracie.' And it happened, and it truly was one of the biggest surprises of being part of the World's Fair. You'll never guess - Being invited back to Morton. After the PTA not wanting me to do the Follies anymore, and all the hell I had gone through to survive the nineteen years, I'm invited back! And I will tell you, damn straight I was going back. Portland and the whole Rose Festival Association didn't want me, but my folks did. And I wanted to show all of those in the press, that Gracie goes where she is wanted and does what she says she's going to do. I don't do press stunts like the press said I did for that stupid Merrykhana parade in June.

Morton was holding the 20th Annual Morton Loggers' Jubilee and I was invited to be the Grand Marshall of the parade. I was afraid that they would withdraw their invitation, sure I was, but at the same time, I needed the press, I needed the exposure, and I needed some good old-fashioned Morton air. I wouldn't normally say this, but I so wanted to go back and show everyone that even if you are from Morton, you can make something of yourself. Since we didn't do a show on Sundays, it was easy to get some of the girls and acts to come down with me. They shouted at the idea, 'We wanna see where you came from!'

I couldn't resist. So, on Sunday, August 13th, we got into a chartered bus, the load of us and some newsmen, photographers, press agents (Guy and Bob's idea – 'this way they will feel that they have the inside scoop'), a guitarist and clarinetist (Jackie's idea, thank god), and we all drove to Morton. I wore a silver sequined dress. When we got in line for the parade, I got into my '62 Buick Electra 225 Convertible, which was driven down the day before. Placing my feet on the back seat, I sat on the trunk of the car and then was driven down Main. I could not believe my eyes and ears as I was greeted with cheers and adoration – what had I done? I heard, "You look mighty pretty Gracie." and "Good to see you again."

Oh, I saw a few faces that weren't so welcoming, but, I didn't care. Wasn't that why I wanted out of Morton?

They put me at the end of the parade, probably for the most impact. I chuckled, I wondered if the parade watchers were saying, "Where's Gracie?" The morning had some fine mist in the air but seemed to stop as the parade wound through town. But, just like Morton, right in the middle of the parade, there was a downpour! Fortunately, I didn't get caught in it, thank god they put me in the back of the line!

Geez, the whole thing was just terrific. Mom and George came and we were photographed together. It was also good to see my friends, Esther, Melverna, Ross, and the list went on and on. Was Leo there? I do not know. Even if he was, nothing was going to spoil this day.

The Loggers' Jubilee awarded the 'All-American Logger' after competitions of choker setting, power saw buckling, hand buckling, tree topping, log chopping, ax throwing, hand falling, trailer backing, novice speed climbing and speed climbing and, of course, log rolling. After those awards were handed out, I was asked to come to the podium. Well, I knew I was the Grand Marshall, but what I didn't expect was to be awarded the gold ax to commemorate the 20th Anniversary of the Jubilee.

Before I left town we went over to Esther's house and reminisced. Esther is the one were gave me the inspiration and she is the one I owe so much too.

Esther, Melverna or someone had let it slip that the following week would be my 40th birthday. Now, I am not one to celebrate that 'glorious day'. To me it's just a way to watch the clock tick closer to the end and further away from the beginning. So, as I entered Show Street, there stood the cast, crew, the band, and some of the Century 21 guys, and right in front was a big cake. 'Happy 40th Gracie!' I have to admit, even though I hate birthdays, this was very special and I ate some cake and thought, 'they did this for me – wow!'

What is worse, getting a good review or a bad review or getting no review? Well, we had been doing really well with the press until a couple weeks before closing, and then the press started having a bit of fun, *'Rene Fraday and Pierre Guerrin (they're the owners-producers of the famed Paris Lido show)flew into town last week to catch the Gracie Hansen's Paradise International Show. Well, you can only imagine how their presence set the cast all a-quiver (the term is used advisedly here). But the Lido chiefs passed up the bare-bosomed set and all those dancers and went crazy over Bob Williams and his good dog Louie. Bob who's learning French, and Louie who doesn't have to, is opening at the Lido on December 12.'*

All I can say is, at least someone stayed employed after the Fair closed!

As the Fair drew to a close, the crowds started pouring in. We couldn't serve them fast enough. I kept thinking as I stood on stage night after night, 'hey, where were you in July and August when we had practically nobody in this place.'

The press started saying things like 'science might actually beat sex,' and inside I thought, 'if some of these reporters had a little bit of sex, then they would leave us alone.' But, the bills were getting paid, and with full houses and smiles on most faces, I began not to care. To my great relief, now I didn't feel I would need to rob a bank.

It's odd how in moments of desperation you want everything to go away and you forget the good times. And, when the good times happen, you seem to forget the moments of desperation.

All the girls danced harder as the audiences grew, I became braver with my 'Hello, suckers!' Why? I guess it was the fact that I had nothing to lose. I had a captive audience for a few more weeks, then days, then hours. I didn't want to ever forget this feeling of being on this stage, the one I fought so hard to get. I had lived out a dream only a few had been able to realize.

Then on October 20th, Saturday, the neon-lit Apple above the door was turned off.

The End.

1924 - at the age of 2

1935 -Carl, Mary and me

1940 – Senior class photo

1941 – High School graduation

Mary Diana 1938

1941- Mt Rainier, Washington Grandpa Diana, Leo Hansen, me, Jeanette

George and Mary wedding

Mary, George, Carl, me

1961- professional photos of me

1961 – our final
Paradise proposal cover

1961 – Lloyd Lambert told me,
"Rhinestones are just as 'nice'
as diamonds!" (and I agree)

1962- Both photos of me at the World's Fair – Seattle

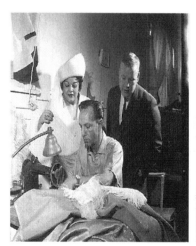 

1962 – me, Barry Ashton
Lloyd Lambert (sewing)

1962 – me @ Hurling Bros.
getting my new "Buick"

1962- Stage at the Paradise International Pavilion where Gracie Hansen presents *Barry Ashton's Night of Paradise*

1962 – The "Famous" exterior of the Paradise International Pavilion

1965 – Outside of the Roaring 20's Room, Portland

1965-67 At the Hoyt Hotel
[left to right Cleo Fast, Bob
Zollars, Howard Butzer]

1965 – by myself on stage

1965 – Portrait of "Gracie"   1966- Backstage @ Hoyt Hotel
that hung over our fireplace

1966 – The Roaring 20's Bar – After a show, all alone in my room

1966- me, Peter Corvallis, Johnny Carson, Anne Francis
Hoyt Hotel- Gracie Hansen's Roaring 20's Room right after
Johnny performed at The Memorial Coliseum

1966 – Portland Rose Festival Parade

1966 photo of Hansen/Cooper family – used for Governor flyer
Left to right – Sam Hansen, Maureen Cooper, Tom Cooper,
me, Bill Cooper (seated next to me) and Tom Jr.

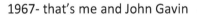

1967- that's me and John Gavin   1967 – Johnny Reitz, me and
                                   Gordon Malafouris

1968- at the Hoyt Hotel

1968 – 4th of July

1970 - Tom Cooper, me

1970- me and Duke Ellington

1970 – Mrs. Tom McCall, Governor Tom McCall and me on election night – "to the best governor money can buy – fondly, Gov. Tom McCall"

1972 – Set of *"Arnie"* TV Show CBS – Herschel Bernardi as Arnie, me and director Don Appel

1973-*The Circle* movie premiere at the Paramount Theatre, me, in middle [unknown left/right]

1972 – Seattle World's Fair 10th Anniversary

Carl, Jeanette, me, mom, George

1980 – Marty Allen and me

2011-Ravensdale, WA
Site of Paradise Pavilion Building

Between Seattle and Portland
The only difference between a rut and a grave is the dimensions

Why didn't we do just one more day? I'm trying to remember now. I didn't even go down for the closing ceremonies – stayed in bed and slept.

Everybody says that I made a lot of money; no, what I did is make a lot of newspaper owners richer by selling papers. Here goes: when the Paradise opened I made $500 a month, then later on $1,000, and then as it was apparent that expenses were going to overreach income, I cut my own salary back to $800. But, for that money I watched over the front of house, made sure the bills were paid, and performed on stage each show, each night of the Fair. So it may sound like a lot of money, but by the end I had less in the savings account than when I started!

Monday, October 22nd. That was a very hard day. I got up as usual, but this time facing the inevitable – cleaning out the building so it could be dismantled. That was so hard. Barry wasn't there, most everybody had left the night before. The sounds of the girls giggling, glasses clinking, everything was eerily silent. I sat on the stage and said, 'what's next, old girl?'

Before I left I looked out into the audience; there sat some seven hundred people for each show, three shows a night, six nights a week for 183 days, a total of 736 performances (okay, that was the way I first saw how it was all going to be and at the closing that is how I could only see it, even though it didn't quite all go according to the estimates); and some of the biggest names I knew – and I entertained THEM! In those seats, watching me were the likes of Carol Channing, Bob Hope, Jackie Mason, Wendel Corey and even Nat King Cole. My biggest thrill was having Mom come and see her reaction. She admitted she 'bawled like a happy baby'. And she told me later that I made her proud – she was proud to know Gracie Hansen.

I have heard that when you reach success, enjoy it while it lasts: I couldn't, as I was working while success was happening. And now that my 'Broadway' debut had ended, who was going to hire me? Ha, certainly not Mr. Chinn. He had told me that he had sunk more than his $5,000 investment; it had totaled almost $90,000 by the end of the run. I didn't expect that to happen, but does anyone expect to lose when you gamble?

Not only did I know how much we lost, the world was going to find out also. Century 21 released that "The Seattle World's Fair, having recorded an improbable triumph of science over sex...ends in black ink...Except for a late rush of business, the Fair's girlie shows didn't cause the kind of stir that Sally Rand's fan dance did at the 1933 Chicago fair...Gracie Hansen's Paradise International, with its bevy of bare-breasted girls, was a moderate success..." At least it didn't say we were in the hole.

For the next week I was in a hospital. Literally. My body was exhausted. I guess I had pushed myself to the point of bed rest. "Tom, the doc said he's not worried, other than if I stayed home I'd be out on the street doing what I am not supposed to be doing. So being in here keeps me pinned down. And besides, I hate this hospital food, I might lose a couple of pounds." I stayed, I gained, I was not happy.

When I got back home, the housedresses stayed on, the kids and Tom saw me more, and I tried very hard not to get depressed. There was no place to wear the false eyelashes, wigs, big earrings, necklaces, rings or boas. A great thing did come out of it, I saw Sambo more. One day I was in the kitchen cooking spaghetti and he walked in, laid his books down and said, "No one understands that real spaghetti has frozen peas in it."

(Okay, I have to say something here. I know it's not proper to make spaghetti with frozen peas – but I love it and I believe to this day, most of the kids will tell you that's how you are supposed to make spaghetti. And to spice it up a bit, add carrots. This way, if someone doesn't like to eat their vegetables, they still get a dose of them in their pasta!)

I looked over at this young man who was so handsome, and I said, "Not everyone is Sicilian. Americans like simple – it's easier on them."

"Are you staying around for awhile or do you have the 'next best thing' coming soon?"

"Son, there isn't 'the next best thing' as you call it. It's what I do for a living, it feeds my soul. Someday you'll find that thing that does it for you."

"Are we all going to stay living like this or what?"

"I think yes." Then I walked over and lifted his chin with my hands and said, "Sambo, you are the one good thing that came out of all those years in Morton. Don't you ever forget that, and that I love you. You are mine and nothing will ever replace you. Do you understand?"

And with that he shook his head a little and then excused himself. Right then I knew that I hadn't given him time that he needed.

But I thought, 'no, you will not regret working, putting a roof over his head and loving him when his real parents would not.'

I lifted a piece of the spaghetti to see if was done and looked into the pot and then thought – 'I'm cooking for six, I hope it's enough.' I stopped and looked around. 'You know, Gracie, you haven't really figured the 'us' in this rented house. Was the 'us' a family or six people living together. Well, the 'living together was something Mom still didn't like. Then I turned down the burner for the pasta to simmer, 'Gracie, take care of one priority at a time.'

During this time, Sambo spent a lot of time at a pool hall on Broadway, up the street from the house. He wasn't just good, he was really good at it. So good that he even got an autographed photo of Willie Mosconi – the famous world champion billiard player, who won fifteen world titles from 1940 through 1957! I didn't like hanging out at the pool hall, well, things happen in places like that. But it seemed that Sambo was really interested in pool and basically stayed away from the trouble.

I have to laugh, but it was sweet also. In the mail came an embossed certificate from the 1962 World's Fair – *Presented to Gracie Hansen in recognition of outstanding service – Seattle World's Fair, Seattle Washington 1962*. I got it framed and hung it up next to my Dale Carnegie certificate.

During the Fair a theatre group came up and asked if after the Fair I was doing anything. I told them that I hadn't really thought about it, and they asked if I'd like to be in their upcoming spring production of *Harvey*. I told them yes, as I thought all I would have to do is tell a joke or two, but just yesterday in the mail I got the script. I don't just tell a joke or two – I have lines, a lot of lines!

Do you know the play *Harvey*? Well, obviously I didn't and well, let me tell you what I learned. Harvey is this rabbit in the mind of Elwood P. Dowd, much to Dowd's family's dismay. My character, Dowd's sister, Veta Louise Simmons, finds Harvey's presence quite disturbing, not only because he's invisible but also because Elwood insists on introducing him to everyone he meets. This simply won't do. To put it bluntly, Elwood's eccentric behavior is embarrassing to her social-climbing efforts. Veta decides to save the family's good name by having Elwood committed. (I didn't want Tom to know about this part.) Well, it turns out that Veta is the one who gets committed instead, and the only one to save her is – Harvey? Well, too bad I didn't go see Jimmy Stewart in the movie version, because I would have instantly said no, but by mid December I was trying to learn my lines.

And, god bless the press, when they found out, an article came out in the Seattle PI dated December 1:

Gracie is memorizing lines for a part in the play HARVEY at Seattle Cirque Theater – Feb 6-March 2, 1963. Gracie who resides at 234-10th Ave E ...Gracie will make her acting debut here in Harvey which she'll play Veta, the sister of Elwood Dowd.

I told Tom, "it's in print so you can't take it back. Besides, I've already made my Broadway debut, why not try off-Broadway."

It opened, it played, it closed. It was work. More work than I had at either the Morton Follies or at the Paradise Pavilion. I admire anyone now who can learn all those lines.

Through that show, I was hired to work in Tacoma to host a late-night movie show sponsored by Serta Perfect Mattress. Thank you, KCPQ-TV, Channel 13 for allowing me not to always host the late-night movie, but turn the show into a talk show and other times have girls come in, model some lingerie – hey, I was known as a 'Madame of the Night', I might as well milk it for all it was worth. I once told the press, "It was the late show with gorgeous girls modeling nighties...we sold an awful lot of mulch for one of our sponsors." And to be honest, doll, what we did was present bedtime fashions, food for lovers, named the eligible bachelor of the week and gave away some of my great hats!

I like that when you are hot that you are 'too busy' and we'll call you later; but when the later happens, they are 'too busy' and say 'we'll call you later.' Never happened.

I did enroll in a restaurant management course at the Edison Technical School, tried to put a book deal together about my life so far – nothing. And there were 'meetings' for a 'real television show' – nothing. Mom had heard about an opening at the Ocean Observer in Ocean Shores, Washington. Fortunately, when I got hired they told me that I could write my weekly column and mail it in. It wasn't much pay, nor much work, but a lot of fun. I was the Ann Landers or Dear Abby of Ocean Shores. I'd advise housewives with sayings like *"Raise a little more hell and a little less eyebrow.* I did get a couple letters questioning my ability to write for the paper, and fortunately, I have a quick wit and wrote in the column , 'Honey, when I ran the liquor store in Morton, the back room was busier than a Beverly Hills psychiatrist's - and a lot cheaper.' And along the way came some night club acts and theatre productions at a small radio station.

What hurt the most is seeing a photo of the sign that I had fought Barry over sitting in a dump heap with other junk. That was hard and humiliating. I did try to find a home for the Pavilion show, but nothing materialized. Nothing. Guy told me that I should put it out to the universe, so when I was being interviewed for the play *Harvey*, I told the reviewer, "Look I just recently formed a company, Gracie Hansen Enterprise's with two of Seattle's premiere public relations men – Guy Williams and Bob Karolevitz. One of the possibilities under consideration for the corporation is opening a restaurant theatre in downtown Seattle, featuring (what else) a girlie revue. I have been all over looking at locations. Everything is either two flights up or down in a basement. If I get a place I want to be able to walk in off the ground floor and everything first class."

We also worked up a budget for 'Gracie Hansen presents Gracie Hansen's Blackouts of 1963'. Guy and Bob thought there would be potential to run the show in Portland, Seattle and Vancouver, BC, the budget looked promising:

BUDGET FOR EACH TOWN FOR THE WEEK:

Music – 5 piece Combo	$1,200.00
Star singer (James Dean, etc)	$2,000.00
Animal Novelty Act	$1,000.00
Line of six girls with costume	$ 900.00
Novelty Act	$ 600.00
Novelty Act	$ 600.00
Novelty Act	$ 400.00
Gracie Hansen	$ 2,000.00
One week salary	$ 7,700.00

Cost of each town expenses

Rent	$1,250.00
Advertising	$2,500.00
Tickets, doorman, usherettes, cashier	$ 500.00
Stage hands, etc	$ 100.00
Misc	$ 200.00
	$4,750.00

Recap:

Portland Gross one day (3000 seats @ $3.00) $ 9,000.00

Less expenses, overhead... $ 4,750.00

1/3 show expenses.............$ 2,560.00

$ 7,310.00

Profit...............$ 1,690.00

Seattle gross four days (3,000 seats @ $3.00)

11/17/62

Nothing happened. Why? I am trying to remember now. Look, I could have gotten $2,000.00 a week! I wish I could remember.

There were talks for the Pavilion to be part of the '64 New York World's Fair. In fact, some press was sent out that suggested as much – in Portland, Oregon, the Oregonian newspaper on May 14, 1963 stated: *'GRACIE HANSEN'S SHOW, one of the big hits of last summer's Seattle wingding, will play the New York Fair in 1964.'* It didn't happen. No, my 'competition on Show Street – Les Poupees de Paris – the risqué puppet show did; yep, Syd and Marty Krofft got the gig. I have to laugh though, it's reported that the Fair organizer; Mr. Moses, insisted that bras be put on the puppets and that the sexy posters be taken down off the front doors of the show.'

Holland Fair Enterprises at the New York Fair did contact me to appear on Bourbon Street. You know, I probably won't lose money on that deal, being subsidized by the bourbon people and all – but it's a year away and a lot can happen in a year, right?

Then in 1964 I thought, 'why not use your popularity and run for office- hey, it's a paying gig.' I had a slogan and everything 'I'm not going to open up the town, just your minds.' But that plan shortly had to be dropped...I was told that I was four months short of the required city residency requirement.

Lo and behold, I got wind that there was going to be a new restaurant in Portland, Oregon. Okay, with my track record several years ago I was a bit skeptical, but Tom and I took a trip south, across the Columbia River, and when we drove in I felt like this could be our second home. We drove across the Broadway Bridge and down into what I would consider the skid row side of any town. One newspaper called it "the pearl in the dirty mattress of Portland's skid road." Which, to be honest, wasn't too far from the truth. But then, driving up to the hotel, I loved the gas lights out front, the stained glass that spelled Barbary Coast, and I said, "this just doesn't fit here."

Tom laughed, "then you'll fit right in."

We went in and met the owner, Harvey Dick. Now, I had met Harvey once before, but briefly, but this was my chance to show him that 'no matter what he was putting together, Gracie was his girl.'

The interior of the hotel did not do justice to the outside. There were antiques everywhere and it felt like I had gone back in time, and the 'Madame' that some had called me might actually become a reality.

He showed us the one hundred-plus hotel rooms, the Tiffany Room restaurant, the 24-Hour restaurant, the new Barbary Coast that he had just finished.

"This is all impressive," I said...which it was.

"Well, I am in need of someone to run this room."

I looked around, 'it's not for me. I know I have a degree in restaurant management, but I don't want to just manage."

"I thought as much. After knowing what you did in Seattle, I think it can happen here. I've been thinking about taking that old parking garage out back and turn it into a live stage show room, would that interest you?"

"That's quite a commitment."

"I imagine it will take about a year, but what do you think?"

"Are you offering me to just manage the room, or be part of the room? And, aren't you worried about my reputation?"

He roared with laughter, "You have nothing on mine."

And that's when I knew I had found my second home.

PORTLAND

My motto is that you have to have a singleness of purpose.

I had some input on what the room was going to look like, but for the most part he said, "you'll love it, I guarantee. No expense is too much for this. You wanted your place in Seattle to be a Las Vegas-style joint, well, this place will have everything that Las Vegas has to offer."

I liked Harvey. He was a straight shooting kind of guy who didn't mince words. He seemed a lot like my Tom, a man's man.

"One year?"

"I can't guarantee it, but with everything that needs to be done in that building, it's going to take that long."

Driving back to Seattle, Tom and I talked a lot. Since the room was going to take months to be built, we still had time to figure out our lives. The drop-dead date to be in Portland was March 1st. That meant taking the kids out of school right before spring break and then transferring them to a whole new situation. We needed a place to live. Daddy needed to find a job. Again, he was doing all of this for me. But I also think he was looking for something new as well. When we did tell the kids, there was a split reaction. Mostly, 'why?' It's hard to say to Sambo, 'to find my next best thing.' But that was true, and hopefully it was the next best thing for everyone.

What to pack, what not to? I had so much stuff from the Fair that even Tom acknowledged that I needed a house just for my stuff. I didn't want the kids to feel like my stuff was more valuable than theirs, so we all agreed that keeping only the 'good stuff' was what mattered. I, however, had a lot of good stuff to keep.

One evening, after working his shift and the kids were all in their rooms, Tom came in and said, "Gracie, the kids and I, well, we're making a big move, again, with you and Sambo to Portland. And, before you say anything, hear me out."

I didn't want to stop him; either this was really good news or really bad news. I wanted better-than-average news.

"I don't think you and I should keep 'living together' without making it official. I want you to marry me."

My jaw dropped. We had never once talked about this. Honestly. We just seemed to have brought both families together and with enough patience, love and glue, it worked.

"Marriage."

"It's not a deal breaker, but it really is something that we've been avoiding for about five years. I think the kids, okay, and I, need this."

"Done." I had a man who supported me mentally, more than anyone else. He understood this crazy Sicilian Gracie Hansen, and I didn't think I should let that go.

So we did. We were married at Mom and George's house on March 7. I never thought that I would see my name on a marriage certificate again. Jeanette was there as well. She had her minister from the Olympia Church of Christ officiate. She told me that she had told her minister about our current living arrangement, "Now, they are both divorced and have been living together for the past several years." To which he replied, "There are some things I won't be responsible for." We didn't let anyone know except very close people. This was for us. After the years in the public eye, it just seemed right.

Before too long we rented a house on SE Washington Street; 4410 to be exact. It wasn't what we wanted, but this move was going fast and we grabbed what could potentially fit the family. Yes, I said family. Sambo was in high school and Tom, and Bill weren't far behind. God bless Sis, I always have felt she was the one being left behind by the boys. But she never seemed to complain and I didn't want to push 'Mom' on her; if she wanted it, she'd nudge me toward it.

I started at the Hoyt on March 15th – things were going fast, right? It seemed we just got the kids signed up for school and it was spring break. But I wouldn't have time after work began at the Hoyt and Tom began finding another career – trade school to learn how to weld. He said that the pay was good and it was good to be working with his hands. I liked it, because he could begin to take some of the jewelry pieces I had been collecting and make them into brooches, necklaces and the like. It seemed perfect to me!

On March 24th a large article was published in the Oregonian about me and the Roaring 20's Room. It said a couple things that just weren't true. First, that the room would open late April or early May (add a couple more months) and I was a sturdy little woman. Now what in-the-hell did that mean? It went on to say that the Hoyt was 'a pearl in the dirty mattress of Portland's skid road.' Now that would not have made me want to rush down there and see the place!

I had heard that a Press Club was formed in Portland, and since I was a member of the press, I put in an application. Within days I received a rejection letter, so I asked why. "Listen,

I was a columnist for the Ocean Observer in Ocean Shores, Washington. I'm a member of the National Federation of Press Women, Inc. That should put me a little closer to the Fourth Estate than some character selling cars or advertising." Well, the newspaper caught wind of this and then asked Ronald Schmidt, public relations man and President of the club, if this was true. "Look, the membership is limited to radio, TV, advertising men, public relations men, photographers and news reporters. The board of directors just didn't think she fit into the communications field. And besides, hers wasn't the only one rejected."

Not being the only one rejected or not, I fired back and told them that I knew of a jeweler who is a member of the club. "And they have one man who handles advertising for an automobile dealer. I should qualify, I'm selling all the time." I never did get my application accepted. They do not know what they missed.

Things seemed to be going fast in my personal life, but at the Hoyt, it was going terribly slow. I didn't really know what Harvey had planned, —really have planned until it started taking shape. The room was huge — it turned out to have enough tables and chairs to seat 500 people. The tables were from Italy, the chairs were Czechoslovakian bent back, there was a domed ceiling above the stage, and the stage was unbelievable. It was on four hydraulic jacks that lifted and raised. I noticed that the front of the house was turning out as beautiful as anyone could hope, but there wasn't much backstage space. When you have dancers, singers, musicians and me, well, you need a bit of room. Harvey said, "we had to sacrifice somewhere. Tell you what, there's a warehouse across the street, you can have them store whatever they need over there and maybe even have that as a dressing room."

The plaque near the front door read: 'Dedicated to Pleasure'.

Crazy as it sounds, I accepted. I knew of the Seattle rain during the winter, I had hoped that Portland had less – I was to find out that wasn't going to be the case.

The outside of the building had statues on the top that were about 4 feet tall, there was stained glass embedded in the walls, and all I could say was, "there is nothing like this anywhere." And secretly I said, "this is what I should-have had in Seattle after the Fair." But, you can't look on a 'should have' and expect to have it now. No, this was a new adventure, and I was ready for it to happen.

I didn't know the Portland music scene very well, but there were already other 'fine dinner and dancing establishments' such as Amato's and the Ho-Ti. But Harvey kept telling me, "we're going to outshine them all."

It wasn't my money this time, I was just the hired help. So, if he said it, I believed it.

After Memorial Day, I was introduced to Portland's famous band leader, Monte Ballou. He had become pretty big in Portland and even had a hit record. I was to find out later that he thought, and the press was told, that the room was to be called Monte Ballou's Roaring 20's Room. Monte greeted me, a bit cooly, and told Harvey what he was thinking should happen onstage. After he finished, Harvey turned to me and said, "Oh, by the way, I have hired a choreographer for you, his name is John Hillsbury." This was another name I didn't know, but it didn't sound too reassuring.

The next day, John and I met and he said, "so what are we going to be doing?"
I thought for a second about what Monte had told Harvey how the room was going to be run and then I said, "well, it's going to have to be a bit different than Seattle."
"Seattle?"
"Yes, the World's Fair a couple years ago."
"Oh, you're that Gracie Hansen."

I didn't know what that meant, but if I had to, I would work with Monte's music suggestions and work with John on how much choreography I could get. Since the room was called the Roaring 20's Room and Monte's band was called the Castle Jazz Band, I got the Charleston.

I was beside myself.

I penciled out a rundown of the show, John and I auditioned girls and found five dancers led by Ginny Becker, and started running through routines.

Somehow we managed to build a show and have it open on Wednesday, July 28th.

It wasn't quite a disaster, but it wasn't glorious either.

John put the girls through the paces, but neither the dances, the music or the costuming was inspiring. And I want you to know, it is very hard to walk out in front of a crowd of people. Who are waiting to be entertained, no, demanding to be entertained, and you have to entertain them.

We were closed on Mondays so, I took Harvey 'out on the town' and we went to the Ho-Ti Lounge.

They must have known who we were, or at least Harvey (he was known all around town as 'Millionaire Harvey'), because they sat us in the front row. Now, secretly, I was on a mission. I had heard their floor show had $15,000.00 worth of costumes, and some great dancers and singers. I wanted to see the competition. Well, to be honest, it wasn't the 'greatest' but it was a hell of lot better than our show. I sat there embarrassed for what we had. No, not the theatre, but the talent on stage. So after the show, I sent a note back that I wanted to meet the choreographer, director, someone responsible for the show. Sipping on my straw, this slim, elegant young man walked up and said, "Miss Hansen? Mr. Dick? I'm Gordon Malafouris."

After which, he sat down, and out of Harvey's mouth came, "Terrific show, kid. How would you like to come and work for us? We've got shit down at the Hoyt and need your kind of talent."

Did he just say what I was thinking or wanted him to say?

Gordon looked at the both of us and said, "we can talk, but not here."

After drinks, we went down to the Hoyt. Harvey showed Gordon around. "You see, I've had this hotel off and on since '41. But, in the past two years I've poured more than $2 million into this joint – it now has five restaurants and two bars. Here in the men's room, the urinal is a trough with a 10-foot waterfall that cascades over a cliff of a sculpture of Fidel Castro. If you hit Castro's mouth just right, bells and whistles go off. And not to be outdone by the men, in the ladies powder room the fixtures are gold-plated and the lavabos are made of French porcelain."

"This hotel has not only great bathrooms but, a world-class collection of paintings that range from a possible Gainsborough to a genuine Rubens. And look here, a valuable collection of 2,500 miniature liquor bottles and let's not forget the Fotoplayer. It's a turn-of-the century piano – which can recreate the sounds of 17 instruments."

I had to take over, anybody would have run by now. "Gordon, would you like to see the Roaring 20's Room?"

"Yes, please."

This was my territory, and I wanted Gordon. As I walked him around, showed him the state-of-the-art Las Vegas lighting, the hydraulic lift stage, I casually mentioned how much I enjoyed him in the show and how much knowledge he would bring to this show. "This is just the type of thing we need here. In Seattle, we had something ..."

He interrupted me, "I know, I saw it, and I met you, as well."

This isn't what I was expecting to hear. I try to remember people, but I just couldn't. "We've met?"

He chuckled slightly, "Yes, I was doing a show up in Seattle with John Raitt, about the time the Fair opened and we met then."

I nearly fell over."Thank goodness. Those were some hectic times, if I would have met you on more calmer terms, I surely would have remembered you."

"Gracie, can I be forthcoming?" By this time, Harvey had excused himself as he usually did. "My contract at the Ho-Ti has been up for a while. I've actually been contacted to go back east to do a Broadway show."

"Then, what is stopping you?"

"Maybe this. And I also own a store that sells fireplace accessories and it's starting to really take off."

"You are doing live theatre while you are running a full-time company? You are crazier than I am." Was I talking him out of doing this or was I too impressed.

"I'll do it. But…"
There is always those in life.
"I will need to know who is onstage, who is in the pit, and who is in charge."
"I'll make sure of all of it, and if you accept working here, I am the producer, final say, but if the product is good, then you, Mr. Talent, will be the one who can call all the shots onstage."
"It's a deal then."

I think John knew his time was coming, because he showed up the next night and said he had heard that Gordon was brought in, and would we mind him staying around as the stage manager. I wondered why, and he said, "I want to learn from the best." John stayed for about another year, one of the best stage managers we ever had.

That same day Harvey asked to see me, "Gracie, you've proven that your heart is in this place, I'm going to call it Gracie Hansen's Roaring 20's Room…it is all yours from here on out." Secretly I was hoping this going to happen, but to be very honest, I was willing to just be the comic relief if that was what was needed to pull this place together.

It wouldn't be for another couple of weeks before Gordon came, but what happened next was truly unexpected. The dancers and singers staged a strike. They stated that they were not being paid what others in town were, and true they weren't union, and they deserved better pay. I had experience unions in Seattle as everyone was union. In Portland, only the band was union, the actors and stage hands were not. John was not, neither was I. That night, of all nights, a train-full of people from Seattle came down to see the show. Embarrassingly, it was not much of a show.

Here were my people, coming to support me, which they had for several years, and what did they get? Not much.

Somehow we survived the next two weeks, limping along. Gordon was a breath of fresh air. He came in with a smile, he demanded professionalism, and he started finding people who wanted that as well. Amazingly, Harvey left his investment alone. Maybe he knew that it took awhile? Or he truly did know what he had and was happy when Gordon made his presence known. Whatever the case, the show changed; the numbers just seemed to be better, there was an oomph to everything and everyone.
Everyone except Monte Ballou.

Now, maybe it was because he thought that the room was to be called Monte Ballou's Roaring 20's Room, or he didn't like taking orders from this 5'1" Sicilian woman, or and more importantly, Gordon would request that things be done as rehearsed unless it was discussed earlier and agreed that a change was needed. It was getting worse, and it seemed especially so when I was on stage. He would either speed up or slow down the tempo of a song at any given time. I didn't even have to say a word to Gordon: he already knew and at the end of the set would be over talking to Monte. It didn't change.

By February, I was about ready to quit. Hadn't the show gotten better? Weren't the houses full for the four shows a night? And, why was I the target? Anyway, Gordon asked if I was doing anything on Monday. Now, normally on days off the last place I wanted to be was at another theatre. I had a husband and kids who should be watched after. Then he said, 'trust me, you'll be glad you came.'

We went over to the Sheraton Hotel - Lloyd Center and listened to Johnny Reitz and his orchestra playing at a convention. His band was clean cut, as was this adorable man with glasses. I looked over at Gordon – 'we need him.' After the set we sat down together. He was going to go for his broker's license, but if the gig wasn't for very long, he and his band would consider. On the spot Gordon offered him a two-week contract, and he stayed for three years!

Then, when he stepped down, LeRoy Anderson (one of the band members) continued until the Hoyt Closed. But how do we tell Monte? That was a miserable time. It wasn't me who wanted him out, it was that he didn't fit. Gordon kept saying, "we all have to be on the same team. If you can't be a team player, then leave." Well, Monte wasn't the only problem. There had been rumors that Ginny was causing quite a stir on and off the stage. It didn't matter who you are, you do not drink and go out on stage to perform. It is dangerous to you and to everyone else. I finally went to Harvey and told him the situation. "I know you let what happens in the 20's Room stay there, but there is a problem and I need you to intervene." Once I told him the situation, he didn't believe it. It wasn't until one night, he found her drunk and had to help her walk around the building to sober her up.

Gordon asked Harvey if there was a way that we could go down to Los Angeles and buy 'real' costumes. Harvey wasn't quite pleased with that comment. Hadn't he spent a good amount of money on what was on stage?
Gordon agreed, but said, "More sparkle and legs will bring more people." So, we flew down on Monday, went through some inventory and found Ice Follies costumes that were no longer being used. They were amazingly gorgeous. Sparkles where sparkles needed to be, beads, lace, cleavage – the works. We bought the whole lot; shipping them home, though, was another adventure.

Once home, Gordon really started changing the show. New costumes meant new staging and choreography. He would choose songs, put them together on a reel-to-reel and play them during rehearsals, and the girls would rehearse until about 2 weeks before opening, and then Gordon would give Johnny a tape and they would write out the score for the rest of the band. It was great; with the band being union, it didn't put their employment into jeopardy and it made us smarter about rehearsal times.

Our first review came in, December 4, 1965: *'the new revue is actually better than the first one...despite the lack of any major talent, the revues that Gracie Hansen, John Hillsbury and Gordon Malafouris produce at the Hoyt have a number of engaging qualities. The labored chorus brio of chorus line is usually depressing. All those yips of phony gaiety...they don't satisfy on any level. Another good thing about the current revue (it runs through Dec 28) is the considerable employment of Monte Ballou and his Castle Jazz Band...it goes on...and since the "Roaring 20's" crowds aren't the most hip in the world, no one feels that they are being high hatted.'* There was more, but I'm sparing you some of it. It wasn't a good revue and it wasn't bad.

Within seven months we went through a whole band, a whole cast, new costumes, a new choreographer/director – things were always changing. I didn't even have time to really worry about home, until... You see, Sambo was a senior and wanted to go where everyone goes for spring break – Seaside. He had recently purchased a 1957 Chevrolet Bel-Air, which he really loved. Then the phone call – one that all parents dread. It was from the Seaside Police Department – Sambo had been arrested and they wondered if there would be someone willing to bail Sambo out of their jail. I was working that night at the Hoyt, so I'm thinking it was John (Gordon's brother) and Tom went down. This still shakes me up. This is not what I wanted for my son, or for any of the kids, but anyone can have this happen if they drink and drive. When I got home, Sambo was in his room. What do I say? I'm a bad mother for not being here when he needs me? That what I was doing, finding my 'next best thing', was hurting the one I loved? Tom tried to reassure me that it doesn't matter which of the kids did it, it's that any one of them had the potential to do it, and now that it happened <u>maybe</u> the others and Sambo will learn from it. That night as I lay in bed, I remembered the night I married Leo and made Mom so mad at me that I was shoved into the French doors. Were they ever fixed? Who took care of Mom when she lay in bed that night worried at what she had done for me to run off and marry without her consent. I hope Sambo never has to go through this, I hope it ends tonight.

It was summer and the kids were scattered about with various relatives, Sis up at my brother Carl's, the boys up to Bellingham, and Sambo graduated and, wouldn't you know it, his draft notice came. Why is it, right after you get your diploma and are ready to become a member of 'society' that you are called to fight a war that nobody (I suspect a few did) wanted! He went to boot camp, came home for a few weeks and, before you know it, he was shipped out. But not to fight on the front lines, but off to Germany. I couldn't believe my ears, it wasn't Vietnam – it wasn't where many died, he would be safe. My baby would be safe.

I asked Tom if he wanted to come work as a bartender to make a couple extra dollars, and he was more than happy to strap on his over-the-top vests and bow ties I made him and come to the Hoyt. And with that extra money, we bought our very first home together. Oh, Tom had bought one with Beulah in Reseda, CA, with his VA loan, but I had never had a mortgage in my name before, so this would be a first. The house, to me, was huge. Located in the nice Irvington neighborhood – 2628 NE 21st to be exact – I was in heaven.

One house off of Knott street, it had a large porch, big windows, fireplace, large lawn, two stories and a lot of room. I wished we could have afforded this in Seattle while Sambo was living with us, so that the whole family could be in one house, but life doesn't always give you what you want, now does it?
And when Gordon heard about the house, he came over and said, "Gracie, with my help, we can really do this place up." I had

almost forgotten he owned Gordon's Fireplace Shop. Or that each night, he would close the store and just make it to the show. Was this guy crazy?

Okay, are you ready? Downstairs we glued some beautiful pinky-beige brocaded fabric to the walls, and Gordon insisted that the ceiling in the entrance, living and dining room be gold-flecked. He also found this wonderful large oval Alexander Smith Chantilly rug, with a huge black, red and rose floral design. When the kids got home, we all painted all almost 4, 500 feet of molding – it took hours! But, through trial and error we were making ourselves a home. We selected furniture that was specially made in North Carolina and shipped out to us. Was I not living like a Queen? Even our bedroom would make the press jealous; I wanted so badly to say, "boys, yep, I am a Madame and my bedroom can attest to that!" Trig (Helen Tregoning from Morton) came down, brought out the old Singer Featherweight sewing machine, and sewed the red velvet pillows for the couch and my velvet headboard. She was such a clean freak, after she left and we couldn't find anything we'd say we were 'Trigged'.

No one agreed with me to carry the living and dining room theme through the rest of the house, so the gold, red and white stopped there. In the kitchen I had walls painted pink and, keeping the appliances that came with the house, I had some avocado green-flocked contact paper applied to them. Through doing all the work, the kids, the boys especially, kept saying, "I don't want anything like this in my room." For Sis, an eight year old girl, I did what I would have wanted, simple. As you grew older, it could be changed to fit a growing teenager. Her room looked out over the yard and onto the street – so it faced west. That gave me an inspiration, 'let's make it bright'; so the room was painted white, with a yellow bedspread with a large rose in the middle and curtains to match.

Once the inside was done, which took forever, we had the outside painted a dark grey with white trim, then red and white striped awnings. Each night I drove up, I would scream, "I'm home to my castle!"

Gordon asked if I'd like to go to Vegas and see other female performers, one in particular, Miss Totie Fields. You know, I have always been able to relate to Totie. Her weight problem, her image, her love for her man, I instantly said yes. Unbeknownst to anyone, I brought along a tape recorder, and, when I thought no one in our party was looking, I placed it on the table, put a napkin over it and taped her whole show. Why not steal from a genius, right? And besides, who in Portland would know that the material was from her and that she wouldn't know I was 'using it' – you know, 'keeping it warm until she came to Portland.'

Gordon backstage one afternoon while I was sorting my jewelry and said, "Harvey just told me that KGW called."
I just kept on puffing away on my cigarette as I cleaned up my jewelry.
Gordon walked in front of me, "did you hear me? KGW called."
"Gordon, who in the hell is KGW?"
It was like I was a hick from the sticks, because he just fought to get his breath. "KGW is the NBC affiliate here in town."
I dropped the rhinestone tiara I had in my hand, 'You know, the last time I had this kind of conversation was with Esther Lester in Morton, when she talked about me going to the World's Fair. I thought she just wanted us to go. So, if you don't mind, help me out here.'

He put his hands on both my shoulders and sat me down. "Need another cigarette?"

"No, I'm fine."

"Good. KGW called and said they want to do a documentary on you."

"I think I need that cigarette."

It was true. They wanted to do a documentary on me and my 'rise to fame'. The long, long road to 'fame'. So, for about a month they 'trailed' me; at rehearsals, during performances, going to talk at men's meetings, going to buy fabric, they even went back to Morton with me when I received the key to the city. And, they said, once it gets edited, they'd let us know when it was going to air. Well, naïve me, I thought that took just a week or two. It wasn't until two years later when it finally aired.

To be very honest, I was having the time of my life – I was close to having it all: a husband, a family, a home and a job I loved. But the 'next big thing' wasn't anything I did. Do you remember, I said I knew about Barry Ashton because of Variety? Well, guess what, they came and reviewed our show! Can you believe that they came all the way to Portland, Oregon, and reviewed our show?

Tell me what you think: *August 10 VARIETY MAGAZINE:*

"Roaring 20's Revue" with Gracie Hansen, Shelby Howe, Ray Ball & Aggie Lee, Barbara Race, Osa Woodside, Harvey Boys (3), Roaring 20's Dancers (8), Johnny Reitz orch (8), presented by Harvey Dick; produced by Gordon Malafouris; no cover, no minimum weekdays; $1 cover weekends – The Roaring 20's

Room is maintaining its record of producing click shows with this sixth edition layout. Bill is brisk, slick and well executed and should keep the SRO sign up for the duration. Four lavish production numbers, plus several vaude turns, adds up to 50 solid minutes of entertainment.

Shapley Shelby Howe scores with her sock juggling and unicycle work. She has ringsiders gasping as she tosses three saucers and cups to the top of her head from one foot while the other keeps the eight-foot uni-cycle steady. Femme makes the tricks look easy.

Ray Ball & Aggie Lee fill two spots in the session. In the first round they please with some banjo duets. Aggie slams out some better than average standards. Ball displays some rope spinning trickery in the second go-around.

Hostess Gracie Hansen gets belly laughs with her comedy strip number. The Harvey Boys (Stan Choate, Carl Manning, Dean Gordenier) are singers in the Roaring 20's groove with harmonize well. Boys have opera-trained pipes and garner nice returns for their song along.

Barbara Race qualifies in the terology department, with her high kicking Charleston routine. Blond Osa Woodside steps through an interpretive jazz bash.

Production numbers are plotted around "Roaring 20's", "Coney Island" "Hollywood" and finale with big, brassy "Hello Dolly." Six young, clean-cut dancers and two tall, well-turned showgirls register nicely. Costumes are colorful and lighting a plus. Johnny Reitz Orch (8) ably backs the show. Feve. Reprint Variety Aug 17, 1966

And then, the Oregonian ran it with a big headline: GRACIE HANSEN'S ROARING 20's REVUE GETS NATIONAL ACCLAIM 3 TIMES!!!

The Paradise International didn't even get this kind of press – I ran over to Gordon and hugged him, "You are a genius!"

Everyone was ecstatic, except Gordon. I immediately had a flashback to when I put the sign up and Barry got mad. I looked at Gordon, "is something wrong?"
"I'm quitting Gracie."
"No. No! We are a team. You said, if you want to be on the team, stay. Please stay."
"I can't. Harvey won't give me a raise for all the work that I have done."
He turned around and walked away.
I went immediately to Harvey and tried to plead for Gordon. Harvey kept saying, "He doesn't need more money, he's got plenty of it. And besides, didn't I put his name in the ads, folding cards at the table, Directed and Choreographed by... we can find someone else."

I don't if Gordon needed the money or not. Or it was something else that he needed or wanted. But what I knew is that I needed Gordon!

It is said that some of the reason the Roaring 20's Room was successful was because of the cost. For $10 a couple could have a prime rib dinner, have two drinks each, dance and see a floorshow. Which, face it, is pretty reasonable, and some say it's because of me. But I say what made the Roaring 20's Room work was Gordon. Before he came, we were struggling, but look at the full house now!

Harvey suggested I go with Clay Nixon to Las Vegas and see a couple of people who 'might fit the bill'.

While we were there I saw an Eddie Cotton fight – I'm not much into men hitting each other. And then we saw several stage shows, with one directed and choreographed by Rene' De Haven. We're in Las Vegas seeing a Vegas show – so they should be a Vegas show. But, would a true Vegas show do well in Portland? I have finally figured out that the Roaring 20's Room was pretty unique. There were no other types of rooms on the west coast at all like it except for Reno and Las Vegas. But I was also losing Gordon, so it was either go home and do the directing and choreography myself (no thank you), or offer a contract to Rene'. Which we did, and he accepted, on one condition: That he bring up his partner Roc Neuhart and one of his female dancers. Now, I saw the amazing dancing Roc did on stage and that seemed logical, and maybe his female dancer could bring some 'Las Vegas' expertise to Portland. After a couple calls to Harvey, it was agreed. On the way home on the plane, I kept thinking, 'wouldn't it have just been simpler and cheaper to pay Gordon a couple bucks more?'

One of the stipulations to the 'out of town' help was to have them live at the hotel for free. So, after Rene' got settled in, we started preparing for his debut in Portland as director and choreographer. He met the band and Johnny – that went well. He liked the room, how the stage moved up and down and how the tables were laid out, he indicated, 'very Vegas'. When I looked around, I had to agree. The next introductions were with my girls and the boys and that also seemed to go well and then, the costumes. It was like everything stopped. 'I cannot have anyone who works for me wear these rags.'

Did I hear that right? They had worked well during the past year we had them; in fact the audience was still awed by them during the show. I looked at him and thought, he has a contract. "It is what we have."
"It is not good enough. They will do for now, but by the time my show opens, they will be new."
His show?
When I focused, he was gone. What I didn't know is that immediately he went to Harvey and demanded better costumes. And, without consulting me, Harvey agreed!

Again, wouldn't it have just been better, easier, less stress and cheaper to have just paid Gordon what he wanted?

There was a lot of tension between Rene' and myself, but I tried my hardest not to let the cast, crew or band know. It wasn't their fault and besides, some of them had been with the show from day one and maybe I was the one who had to bend a little. I really missed Gordon.

I guess to smooth things over, Harvey thought it would be a good idea for the Hoyt to have a representation in the Merrykhana Parade. It was now called the Starlight Parade, and he asked me if I wanted to be the 'face of the Hoyt'. Well, there I was, sitting in this 1936 Rolls Royce and off we went. The kids, Bill and Sis, were part of it, too. It was fun, no fuss and I looked out over the crowd and thought, 'what would this have been like in '62?'

What happened next goes into my record books of 'oh boy, can you believe this?' Playing as many shows as we did, I never knew who was in town. And with lines now around the block, I didn't even look at reservations. But the flurry of excitement that swirled in the dressing room was amazing. What I thought I heard the girls say was, 'Johnny Carson is sitting at the table near the front side of the stage.' Since Johnny Reitz was our band leader, I just thought they were teasing and I let it go. But, once I stepped out onto the stage and looked over and saw him, I nearly swallowed my microphone. There he was, the famed Tonight Show host, in my theatre, going to listen to my jokes (and ones I ripped off) and sing a couple songs. I made it through the show, and as I always do, changed my clothes and worked the crowd. Not only was THE Mr. Carson there that night, but the beautiful Anne Francis as well! God bless Peter Corvallis from the press, he was there snapping photos. It is one of my cherished moments.

You know, there were times I just simply adored Harvey and then there were times I threatened to kill him. Not only did Johnny Carson come, but others as well. And Harvey never got involved with the Roaring 20's Room except he had several strict ideas that he would not change at all. Cash was the only item of currency – ever; men wore suits and ties and women wore only dresses. 1966 was on the cusp of the pantsuit craze, I wore them now and then, but at that time, they weren't a big part of my wardrobe. Well, one night the wonderful dancer Juliet Prouse came to see our show, wearing what I heard was a very tasteful pantsuit. Janet at the front desk turned her away and, then when she asked to see the owner or manager, Harvey appeared. He told her, the house policy was that if you weren't wearing a dress you weren't allowed in. She turned and walked out. When I heard about this, I went out and found some used men's jackets and ties, bought some of those wrap-around skirts, took them home and Sis and I scrubbed them to make them look presentable. I had them at the hat check room 'just in case' this happened again, and it did – a lot.

The Roaring 20's Room wasn't just for fun and frolicking. I also used it to raise awareness and money for various charities. Gordon told me that John Gavin was coming into town to promote his latest movie with Julie Andrews – Thoroughly Modern Millie - and that opening night of the film would be a fund-raiser for the Multiple Sclerosis Society. So somehow, and you know honestly I cannot believe we pulled this off, we arranged for us to pick up John at the airport, take him in an old Rolls-Royce that Harvey had, and drive him to the Eastgate Cinema and then after, bring him to the Roaring 20's Room where there would be a meet and greet. We knew that the Rolls had an emission problem and the fumes were coming up through the floorboards. From the airport we went to the Hoyt Hotel and had a cocktail. John said, "I can't ride in that car – it smells really bad, I'm taking a taxi." So off we went, and John followed us. When we arrived, throngs of people came over to the car, excited and expecting to see John - poor John was left out in the cold. I laugh now, but, he could have rolled the windows down and suffered with us for the art!

During our conversations, John told me that he was Janet Leigh's boyfriend in the movie *Psycho*, which, I had totally forgotten, I'll need to watch that movie again. Or not. That movie scared me the first time.

Fortunately for me, the Seattle press did not forget me. They came down to interview me and find out if I might come back to Seattle. Well, the one thing buying a house does for you, it stops you from moving around. The kids seemed pretty happy, Sambo was gone to the military and, with Tom bartending once in a while as well as his regular job, we all seemed to have put down roots. In Portland, a city that didn't want Gracie – because I was 'too racy'. They should see me when I'm not outside my house. No makeup, slippers, a kaftan, cup of coffee and a cigarette. What a life.

Anyway, I told the reporter that I was considering coming back to Seattle with my girlie show, but it all hinged on the extension of the Saturday night liquor curfew, which was about to go into effect on August 20th, in less than two weeks. 'Sunday liquor is not as important as some people think. But Saturday night is pretty important as far as show business goes. I'll be watching this with great interest. Remember, it's only 40 minutes and $13.00 by plane between Portland and Seattle. I'm a big spender, doll.'

That got some tongues a-wagging. So much that I was invited to be Grand Marshall of the Lake City's Gay 90's Parade. One article said I wore '30 yards of white ostrich feathers plus 10 pounds of rhinestones.' I guess for a woman small as myself, that's a lot?

And, onstage, things just seemed to roll. For the first time in my life I was comfortable in my skin. I read a lot of joke books, listened to my Totie Fields tapes, and started finding a voice that wasn't just about jokes, but about life, and people liked it. 'I worked seven years in the bank, doll. I found the only way to make money working in a bank is to steal it!' ('I'm somewhere between 40 and death.' 'Because when you get to be 40 you've lost your hair, got a pot belly and five kids.') 'Until you're 40 you make love, after that you make money.' (I think I stole that one). And because it seemed like everyone liked the fact that I came from a town called Morton (it does sound unusual, doesn't it) I'd say, 'I love every minute of it , being here in the Roaring 20's Room- It sure beats the hell out of Morton!' When they laughed, I would laugh with them. And I meant every word of it. It was harder over 40. I was heading the other direction fast. Having the kids growing up didn't help matters either. I noticed just how time raced a bit faster especially when I saw this sad looking creature looking back at me in the mirror. I always wonder why Red Skelton did the clown at the end of the show. Do you remember? When, in just a pool of light, he would 'mop up the light' and then it went out? I think I get it now.

It's true, I have always said, 'Too many people get to be 40 and they have a bald spot and a mortgage and five kids and they think it's too late to do the things they used to dream about.' But I was fat and 40 and I came out of the hills and I made it. My message is this: 'if I could, who the hell can't?'

I started writing my thoughts down. I thought, 'look at all the old gals who are making it big – here is Mrs. Miller, Phyllis

Diller and Gracie Hansen. We were all frustrated housewives.' And I do consider myself just a housewife. I love to cook, hate to clean- HATE TO CLEAN (just ask Tom, the kids or any good friend of mine) and I don't have time for hobbies (I still have that Singer Featherweight sewing machine I bought in Morton all those years ago – and if I get the time, I'll sew something; that's not a hobby, that's my entertainment). I like staying busy. I think that boredom is the curse of the American woman. And I also believe that so many women are bored because they have nothing to do and nothing to look forward to. They can't even look forward to having sex, that's how bad it has gotten.

I did stay busy. For awhile I was in negotiations to do a weekly TV program called 'Gracie and Friends'. But it didn't go very far, so the editor at The Community Press newspaper called me and told me, 'why not make it a column?' And I did.

Every town has celebrities; Portland was the home of some famous people as well: Sally Struthers (All in the Family); Doc Severinsen (band leader for Johnny Carson); Lindsay Wagner (Wonder Woman); Sam Elliot (just a hunk), Johnny Ray, among others. I would go to their homes, or their parents homes, interview them, take a couple photos and then a week or two later, the article appeared in the paper – sort of like the Ocean Shores newspaper with a Hollywood twist.

Now, you know I've said that I hadn't been involved too much in the kids' lives, but, at a request of the Alameda School's Principal where Sis was attending, I was asked to go to her school and help with the school lunches, kinda 'Parent's Day'.

Okay, here goes: Gracie's day at school:

I received a call from a gal who scheduled parents to help out at the school. They liked to involve the parents by having them monitor the playground, lunchroom, etc... She wanted to know, would I be able to come to the school the next day and help out during the first lunch period, when the 1st through 4th graders eat their lunch.

"And what time might that be?"

She replied, "You'll need to be at your station no later than 11:15."

"AM?"

The lady laughed, "of course. So, is it a yes?"

How could I say no, right?

I thought, 'Oh boy, trying to look at doing anything before noon is quite a task.' Then, I thought...geez, why not? This could be fun! I might even make it in the school bulletin, and when was the last time that ever happened?

It was agreed that I was needed selling milk, and then I said something I never thought I'd catch myself saying, "I'll see you at 11:15 AM tomorrow – this is quite exciting."

Now, I need to let you know that Sis took the early lunch, so it would be me selling the milk to her and all her friends. And I wasn't going to let the cat out of the bag to anyone in the house – I didn't know how she would take it, but I was going to be her lunch-time surprise.

Since I didn't get home from the Hoyt until 2 or 3 in the morning, I tried all day to prepare myself to get out of there on time, in bed and get a little sleep.

And would you believe it, I woke up at 9:30 AM. Things sure look different, (myself included), at that time in the morning. So, after pouring a cup of coffee, I started to get ready. What to wear or, should I say, what NOT to wear, and then the makeup. I figured that wearing my stage face wasn't exactly the look any child or parent would like to see when they purchased their milk, but the outfit I chose was a little jazzy, with a few well-placed rhinestones 'cause ya gotta have a bit of sparkle', but absolutely no feathers.

I was actually having fun. Sipping my coffee, having a cigarette and just getting to see what it felt like being a day person. Now don't get me wrong, I wasn't going to do this every day.

Looking in the mirror I thought, 'this is pretty hard' – you know, figuring out what was day and what was night...but, that was while I was gluing on my signature false eyelashes and smacking my lips once more with tissue paper. I grabbed a great wig (can't go out without one!); added some jewelry, rhinestones of course - just a few smaller than usual "diamond" pieces. Grabbed my favorite mink - the color is called "autumn haze"...love that coat, goes with everything. One of the small gifts I gave myself shortly after the Seattle World's Fair ended.

Got down the stairs, looked at my watch and saw that, 'all done and it's just 11...wow not bad.' Took one last look in the mirror, giving that head-to-toe last look, then I stopped, 'too much?' I found myself chuckling...'actually, it's just right.' And off I went. The school wasn't that far away, and fortunately for me, I found a parking space close to the front door, almost like Doris Day did in every movie she was ever in, and I traipsed on up the walkway. I opened the front door, looked at the clock and was pleased to see I was three minutes early. I'm not known to be the most punctual person, just ask anyone who really knows me. I can be counted on to show up at least 15 minutes late. I have been accused that 'it's all about making a grand entrance' and I say, "that, or sometimes it's alright to be 'fashionably late'."

Today was different, I wanted things to go just right and 'tardy' wasn't going to be part of today's vocabulary.

After introductions, I was led over to the table that was all set up for me with a cash box, crates of little paper cartons of milk and a chair which I didn't think I would use, but it was great to put my purse and coat on...I was ready, open for business.

I was looking over my stuff, and thinking how great it was that I had worked in a bank and all that experience with money was going to pay off, but then when I opened the cash box, there wasn't anything but coins. I chuckled, 'think you can balance at the end of my shift!'

Just like clockwork, the kids started filing in, slowly at first. Some from the neighborhood came over and I chatted with them. Then, the real rush started – kids with their homemade lunches waiting for me to sell them their milk. I couldn't help but overhear all the whispering going on among them. Kids at that age haven't learned how to whisper without everyone within ten feet hearing every word they say. These are a few of their 'whispers' I heard, "Look at all her diamonds" "Oh, she must be rich" "Who is she?" "Whose mom is that?"

Boy, I was causing quite a stir and was I ever getting a kick out of all of this!

Those kids who knew me got the word out to the others who I really was. Then I saw Sis. She smiled (I think she was surprised, bewildered, but overall pleased I was there) at the same time trying to answer questions that were being thrown at her, like, "is that your mom?" What I heard her say was, "yeah, she is".

When Sis got up to buy her milk, she realized that she had forgotten it in the locked class room. To her surprise and mine, I had some spare change and proceeded to pay for her milk.

Was she embarrassed? Probably a little, not that I was her mom, or that I was there that day, but I think kids just don't want anyone to know that they even have parents.

All in all I'm glad I was there. First, to be part of Sis' life, but also it's always nice to be reminded how the 'early birds' live, especially if you are a 'night owl.'

I helped clean up and it seemed that the other mothers and the faculty were genuinely nice to me and thanked me for taking time out of my 'busy schedule'. Some mentioned that they had even been down to see the show at the Roaring 20's Room.

Driving away, I thought, I don't think that was too much of a shock for them, but I bet you I gave them all something to talk about!

Business was slowing down again so much so, that we started doing only three shows a night instead of four. Again, Harvey wanted to get 'the face of the Hoyt' out in public, so the Rolls was decorated with pink flowers, the girls got all dressed up and we rode in the parade – the Grand Floral Parade – the second largest next to the Pasadena Rose Parade. What I didn't know is that in 1964 the old Rolls won second prize in the 'Special Commercial Division' category and that he wanted to win again. We didn't, but what I won was the respect of the crowd. We had a great time that day, all the girls from the Roaring 20's Room and I being driven around in the Rolls and also on television. By then, the parade was garnering local and national press coverage – I don't know if we were shown, but the crowd that saw us wind through Portland certainly did.

Tom came backstage with a newspaper in hand, which was truly unusual for him. It was sort of understood that the stage and whatever happened on it or around it was my territory. So, with a bit of surprise, he kissed me and said, "This will just take a minute," and laid the paper in my hand.

I looked down and there was the television listings for the night. "Are you trying to tell me that you'd rather be home watching TV than being here?"
"Tonight I would, yes. Look at the 10 o'clock hour."
And there it was – "10 pm (Ch. 8) KGW Special..." I about froze... *Don't Throw Stones A gentle and humorous examination of how a housewife from Morton, WA, became a regional show business celebrity known as Gracie Hansen.* I turned and hugged him, "two years waiting for them to edit it."

Gordon had been in touch with KGW and their producers. They had gone through hours and hours of tape and whittled it down to twenty-eight minutes. He didn't even know that they were going to show it that night, but the next Monday, a big brown box arrived at his store and inside was the reel of the show.

For several weeks after that, the houses were filled to the brim. Was it because it aired right after school started and everyone was home on a Saturday night in September, or was it because I still had 'the stuff'.

And with the houses being full, and the men running out and telling others about the 10' urinal/trough and the statue of Castro (and the trough was filled with all these plastic plants so if you didn't know that's where you were supposed to pee you'd miss out! and the sit-down toilets were fitted with a coin slot – you had to pay 25 cents to use them – I can just imagine how some people felt trying to figure out the bathrooms – I think the tours helped solve some of the problems) and then women talking about how luxurious their restroom was with the marble, the gold and the fur-lined toilet seats, I started taking people on tours. No charge, just for fun. More of the 'experience of the Hoyt.' I mean, there was a lot to see. Harvey had a chastity belt on display in the lobby, in the Men's Bar (only for men) he had a painting that was covered by a curtain, and only those 'lucky' enough were allowed to see behind it. And what was behind it? A painting of a man sucking on a woman's bare breast. So why not the "tour of the toilets". People asked me, both men and women, when it was going to happen. It all went well, until we had a group of Elks at the 11 o'clock show and someone got mad and then Harvey got a talking-to, and when it got back to me, he wanted to stop all 'toilet tours'. I told him, it's just a place to pee, we all have them in our homes, we've just got fancier ones here at the Hoyt and they should be seen. Nothing more was said, and the 'tours' continued.

Harvey was always trying, like me, to get 'the next best thing'. So, not only having the hotel full every night, all night, and people waiting out in the cold, he wanted to add something else to the mix. He started booking the likes of Harry James. I knew Harry because of who he had been married to, Betty Grable. If I could have had legs like hers – you can only do just so much with a 5'1" body, right?

This wouldn't be the first or the last of the big bands to come through town – Woody Hite, Al Hirt, Wayne King, Glenn Miller band led by Ray McKinley, Donald O'Connor, John Gavin, Count Basie, Buddy Rich. The joint was jumping and everyone seemed to be having a good time. And it must have been because one reporter stated that the whole Hoyt Hotel with the restaurants and bars were 'cracking', as he put it, 500 bottles of whiskey – a night!

Harvey kept telling me that 'the best advertisement was the stuff you don't pay for, but that makes the biggest splash.' So with that I accepted being part of the Gay 90's parade in a small town west of Portland – Forest Grove. I got press, a photo and new fans in this rural place. Looking around I felt like I was back in Morton. *The Gay 90's parade at noon Feb. 22 will feature floats, old cars, horses and bands. Portland's Gracie Hansen will be parade grand marshal.*

Because of Sambo being in the military, Tom serving as a Merchant Marine on a ship taking supplies to the Far East, India,

Malaysia, Burma, Singapore and Da Nang (Vietnam), I started doing my shows on the road. I took the girls with me; they would entertain the troops as only women can and then I came out.

Through this I received a military citation from the Marine Corps. One of the proudest accomplishments I have achieved. Everyone looked at me and only saw the false eyelashes, big wigs, loud dresses, the boas, feathers and all the rhinestones, but what they got was a good laugh, they got to forget about their troubles and I got to be the Northwest version of Bob Hope.

I was so happy to see Tom when he came home, but what happened next was not what I was thinking would happen – he suffered a heart attack. Unfortunately, more would follow, but his first one landed him in Physicians and Surgeons Hospital in NW Portland for well over a month. It wasn't that far from the Hoyt so that helped, but here he was struggling, and with him gone for a year, and now in the hospital for what would be a whole month, I was the only breadwinner and parent. When you have two teenage boys and a young girl blossoming, and you are working full-time, all you can do is see your world spin out of control.

How we survived that time, I will be honest, I do not know. That's when I wanted the housekeeper from Seattle – but where was the money going to come from? I worked every day without a day off, and the money basically stayed the same. And when Tom did come home, it took forever for him to get back on his feet. The hospital bills piled up and so did the problems at the Hoyt.

First, Johnny was leaving to pursue his career dream of being a stock broker; fortunately Le Roy Anderson, one of his band members, was going to take over. Then Rene' was having problems in his offstage relationship with Roc. And then Harvey raised the fee to get into the room. "we've got to raise the money somewhere to run the place." I kept saying to anyone who would listen, "the show isn't that good to keep raising prices to get in – raise the prices of the drinks or a menu item." No one listened.

One funny thing that helped was, when we had the Marquis Chimp act on stage. One night we noticed Marquis he wasn't himself and I think it was Donna who said, "Gracie that guy has tipped the bottle." He went on stage, fell down and spilled the jelly beans he used to reward the chimps when they did their trick correctly. My lord, there they all were, Marquis and his six chimps all scrambling around on stage – some chimps had roller skates – trying to get the jelly beans. Well, the audience loved it, but we were in a panic. So I decided that each night before his performance I would hypnotize him. Thank goodness the acts rotated every three weeks.

Then, Variety came again. Twice? Once was unreal, twice was so amazing to me, I reread the article over and over; even with so many things up in the air, the article was so positive, the show started picking up steam again. The review read like this: *Roaring 20's Port. Portland, Ore. Oct 22. "Toujour Les Femmes, " with The Colstons (2), Gracie Hansen, Jan Brinker, Jo Anna Burns, Howard Butzer, Newhart and LeBrun, Roaring 20's*

Dancers (10), Roy Anderson Orch (8); presented by Harvey Dick; produced by Rene DeHaven; lighting, Ted Halperin; costumes, Ruth Dorette, Janet Hopper; music, Dave Boden $2 cover weekends.

The plush Roaring 20's Room, the northwest's ace entertainment dispensary, enters the fall season with a new show that should keep the 500 seats filled regularly by until new bash bows Dec. 17. Colorful framework remains the same, but specialty acts change every three weeks. The new 80-minute spectacular has the type of flash, flair and femmes that scored so well with auditors during Rene De Haven's previous outings.

The Colstons (2) score big with their "Nut most In Comedy." Guy gets loud laughs with his short standup monolog. His petite sister centers, and 10 minute of hilarious comedy ballroom antics follow. George is a good foil for his loose-limbed mugging sister Arlene. Pair are fine dancers, and garner solid mitting with their contortions, pranks and knockabouts.

In the first show, Arlene in golliwog costume is handled well by George and another sister. They became the Leema Trio and toss Arlene's pliable body around with amusing results. Both acts are tops and suitable for all media.

Blonde Jan Brinker provides the sex touch to the show, and displays her well-stacked chassis. Much improved chirper warbles some old standards for good results, but audiences get away from her during needless talk sessions. Room is too big and act too loose at this point.

Newhart and Le Brun are on for a sizzling adagio turn. Hostess Gracie Hansen grabs yocks with "I'm Perfect." Jo Anna Burns is a little girl with a big classical voice. The pixie singer gets an excellent report card for her song along. With more stage experience and management, she could go far. Howard Butzer

*clicks with above average singing. He teams with Miss Burns for
"Stranger in Paradise" and some "Oklahoma" tunes for a
winning stint.*

*The Roaring 20's Dancers (eight girls, two boys) are on for three
big, brassy production numbers plotted around "Oklahoma"
Oriental and French themes. Terpers are well disciplined, work
hard and move well. Lighting, costumes and choreography are
outstanding. Feve.*

Getting that kind of a review once brought folks in, the second
time, two years later, droves came. For the fall, we were doing a
brisk business. Even if nights faltered, Harvey wasn't shy about
putting ads in the local paper for Mother's Day, Father's Day,
Easter, St. Patrick's Day, Thanksgiving, Christmas and New
Year's Eve. With the show being changed every twelve weeks,
the themes could be built around the ads. The problem was that
the dancers and singers changes as well. And even with
advertising, new shows, changes in songs and dance routines,
there were nights that were slow. I marveled that in a town the
size of Portland we could fill a 500 seat house with three shows
a night – six nights a week. As time went on, it was very clear
there would always be several nights a week that a stage
production that we had been doing for the past several years
was not going to draw. What we came up for the slow nights
was special events. On Tuesday night it became 'Queen for A
Night', where someone in the audience would become Queen
of the Roaring 20's Room for that night. I went out and
gathered all kinds of prizes from various companies – luggage
from the Portland Luggage Company; box of chocolates from
Van Duyn's; a jeweled box from Gordon's Fireplace Shop; and I
even got Red Garter Perfume from Bazar. But the biggest prize
was an Admiral television set.

The advertisement read: *Free parking at the door. Toss your
name in the hat for the 'Queen Drawing.' Receive red carpet
treatment, diamond-studded crown, scepter and prizes, prizes,*

prizes. (You're all invited to go on the famous 'Ladies' Tour of the Men's Room' of course).

This was a lot of work, but it paid off, and we did it for several years. And on Sundays, we had special meetings, conferences, dinners and even drag events. I had been told by many that I was an inspiration for several drag queens. They would say, "what, you are the only one with the corner on rhinestones and boas?" This was a whole new world for me. I had known many gay men over the years. I suspected that Barry was; of course Rene' was, especially when you tell everyone that you 'won't take the job unless your partner can join him as well.' But, they weren't drag queens. I think that's what is great about this business, it allows those who have talent to shine, and to be creative, and it's so liberating to be you- whoever and whatever that may be.

I received a call from an organization that wouldn't give the front desk their name, but wanted to meet with me about booking the room for Halloween night. Now, this year Halloween was on a Thursday, not a huge night to give up, but this had to be some event and the money had to be good. Sitting down with two young gentleman, they began to tell me how they were from the 'Imperial Rose Court of Portland'.
I started to laugh and they started to get nervous. "Don't worry, it's that the Rose Festival and I have had a long, complicated history."
"No, we're not from the Rose Festival, we're separate from them. We host a drag ball each year to crown the new "Empress.""
"So, we won't be crowning the Rose Festival Queen then, will we? Or not that kind of queen."

They chuckled a little, and to smooth things over I told them that we would be delighted to hold the ball here. When I told

Rene and Roc they seemed a bit surprised, but at the same time I told them that I was asked to be part of the festivities. That night turned out to be so much fun. I was sharing my dressing room with men who wanted to be just like me. Why, I had no idea; but they were having a hell of a good time with 'everything'. And I do mean everything. There were more of those nights to come, I got other requests to have drag balls at the Hoyt. I told everyone, 'no more good week or weekend nights, Sunday's only.' And the bookings began.

One night Roc came over to me and asked if there was any way that his 'guest' could borrow a gown. Most of the everything was placed in storage during the week, I told him there wasn't much except what was hanging in the dressing room and that was mine. He sheepishly asked if they could use one 'just for the night.' Well, what the hell, I don't get asked very often for a man to use one of my dresses, but when his 'guest' came in through the door, my jaw dropped. Here was this slender, tall, knockout of a guy, and he was going to wear one of my dresses? "Gracie, this is Walter, Walter Cole. He owns the Dumas Tavern down on 3rd Street, not far from here."

The more I looked at him, the more I couldn't believe this was going to happen, he was the one that interrupted me, "we've met before, after I close up shop, I come up here to the 24-Hour to have breakfast on the way home, about the same time you all eat. You don't mind do you?"

To be honest, I had to see this for myself. Was I mad? Yes, at the thought of using one of my dresses to dress a tall, slender man, but then no, because I was intrigued. "Have you ever worn a dress, wig, anything before?"

"No ma'am, this is a first." What I didn't realize was, I was partially responsible for Walter becoming a drag queen for the rest of his life that night.

Being asked to take my show 'on the road' always was a thrill. I had worked up a name for the show, calling it *Gracie Hansen's Centennial Revue*. This was also due impart because Tacoma was celebrating its 100th birthday. We were asked to come up and celebrate – there was a standing-room-only crowd of about 500 people in the Crystal Ballroom at the Winthrop Hotel – we did that two Monday nights in a row. One thing I have always said is you have to show the boys in the audience great girls with great legs. But what surprised me the most is, when I stepped on stage they went wild. I guess it helped when I said, "I'm Gracie Hansen and I'm one of the bigger unknown stars." Which, being close to Seattle and everything that happened at the World's Fair – they lapped it up. Then I went on to tell them that I was feeling a little nauseous from receiving a letter from Longview High School – to come to the high school reunion. I think everyone can relate right? It felt like I was Johnny Carson doing the Tonight Show – nothing I said went wrong. I had the best time, and it was great being part of the celebration. We did two shows that night. Maybe I should have moved down to Tacoma after the Fair? Who knew I had such a loyal audience there?

Within a few months things turned sour. Janet (who worked the front desk and managed the Barbary Coast Restaurant with Bob De Lozier) was also dating Harvey. She started pushing more and more to take over the Roaring 20's Room as well. "You don't need Gracie, it would run smoother without her."

And when I went into the hospital because I wasn't feeling well, she started taking over my routine.

I heard so many reports that things were bad, that they were going to do a whole routine around a young dancer by the name of Julane Stites. She was talented, so talented that the hopes of building a show around her vanished when she was cast in a Broadway show. And then one night while Roc and Le Burn were doing their routine, I guess the floor didn't go level all the way. As he was close to the edge, he slipped, hitting his back on the edge and had to be rushed to the hospital. The old man fired him right after that. He was one of our best male dancers, too. Things were not going well. Being in the hospital didn't help my health at all. I found out what I already knew. I had diabetes and I wasn't taking care of myself. This wasn't news to me. I found out that I had diabetes when I lived in Morton and had to send urine samples up to Virginia-Mason Hospital in Seattle. It's hereditary. Mom has it, Jeanette has it, Aunt Jo died from it and I believe even grandma, so guess what was knocking at my door. The doctor told me that I had to eat right, rest and try to figure a way to have less stress in my life. He didn't know who he was talking to.

What I did know was that I needed to get back to my insides. Something that I hadn't done since studying metaphysics in Morton, I just didn't have any time. And since I was the one laid up for a week or two and everyone was out of the house, I started thinking and writing and thought I'd do some shopping. But shopping for things is not what I was doing today, today, I was shopping for someone. I am not someone who is good with names, what I have to do is go and see the person, know that's the one I want to chat with and then hopefully during the conversation, they will say their name. Anyway, I headed over to this carpet store near Lloyd Center and fortunately, there he was. He walked right up to me, and said, "Hi Gracie, I don't know if you remember me, I'm John Lane." He always intrigued me as he always remembered who I was and invariably he would say, "Gracie, today your color is..." and off he'd go. Or he'd say, "you have a cloudy aura." I needed him for my latest project. So, once I found out that it was almost time from him to get off work, I told him I'd like to chat with him, and that I'd be over at Sears in the coffee shop if he cared to chat. Not more than half an hour and John was sitting across from me, and by that afternoon we agreed to work on a book together. It sounds crazy, doesn't it? He probably accepted because he liked my aura that day or I wasn't cloudy...

Anyway, that was the birth of what became *Gracie Hansen's Horoscope for Swingers.*

Then one night when Tom and I went out to see Gordon at his home on Blue Lake (which is east of Portland in Troutdale), I told him what had been happening. He told me to quit, and I told him that is easier said than done.

Sitting around his pool, which overlooks the lake he asked me, "what is the one thing you have wanted to do that you haven't done."
"I think I'd like to try my hand at politics. I'm so desperate for money, hell, I'd be the best governor money could buy."
"That's your slogan!"

Tom joined in, "you're kidding, right? Gracie, here, run for governor of what?"
"This is too perfect. Gracie, you are a Democrat, right?"

"Yes, unlike you, Gordon, I'm too poor to be a Republican."

"We'll use that, too."

"What? Use what?"

"Look, the Democratic field isn't very strong this year, the lead contender is Bob Straub. In my book he doesn't have the appeal that, but you have."

"You're serious, you really think this can happen?"

"Why not. This is the '60's – why can't a woman be in an elected office? And, even though I'm a Republican, I'll be your campaign manager and handle all the press."

And, just like that, it was decided that I was going to throw my hat into the race for Governor of Oregon.

Tried-and-true Tom heartily agreed.

As Gordon was filling out papers, I was talking to the old man – Harvey. He was thrilled with the idea. "More press, Gracie, more press, brilliant! I'll throw in one of the rooms here so you can have a campaign headquarters, you can have your big 'coming out party' here as well."

It felt like old times. Gordon chartered a bus, and a group of people, mainly those from the Hoyt, and the kids headed down to Salem to officially register my bid to become the first woman governor of Oregon.

The bus had a large banner on the front: *The Gracie Bandwagon*. It reminded me of the day back in August, 1962, when we all drove from Seattle to Morton for the 20th Anniversary of the Jubilee. There were signs of support: 'Vote for Gracie, keep Oregon Green'; 'Gracie, the Working Man First'; 'We Luv Gracie'.

As I submitted my papers, I said, "Some people will claim I am doing this for a laugh. Well, a little laugh now and then never hurt anyone. I feel I am as qualified as any other of the comedians who are running for public office." I went on and said, "I don't understand why Tom McCall raised liquor prices – just to get the state's welfare system out of the red? What good will it do to raise the price of booze to increase welfare funds when many of the welfarers buy the booze they can't afford in the first place! Besides, we need a good, inexpensive belt now and then to ease the pain of the tax burdens."

Then, the next day, Gordon arranged a press conference in the Tiffany Room of the Hoyt to announce my candidacy. The girls from the show put on small outfits and gas masks (thanks to my statement about President Nixon and dumping), and I announced that I WAS the best for the job. Afterwards, I was surprised not only by the reaction of the press (which was positive), but the staff had made me a *Gracie For Governor* cake. Here's a bit of my speech, *"This is a Red Letter day I have already mentioned to you. For some time I have had my eye on Tom McCall's seat- which is a great deal more than he has had on it. ...I have, therefore, chosen this time to toss my wig into the ring and seek election as Governor of this great State. It seems to me that the present administration has done its thing – and that 'thing' is to create an economic situation that's worse than any woman's checkbook ever thought of being! I'm all for liberalism – liberal arts, liberal education, liberal welfare, liberal morality – in fact, I'm probably the most liberal candidate seeking office today. I feel that the logical and liberal approach to Oregon's tax and economic problems is a very simple one. Why not a State lottery or sweepstakes? From the various 'games people play', from wickey wackery dollars in service stations plus dishes, glasses and flag games, supermarket bingo and bingo in churches, green stamps and dialing for dollars on the radio – not to mention horse and dog races, all form of lottery, it appears that we are all willing to take a chance on chance. If you have read the new book, 'The Selling of the President', then you know that political candidates are sold to the public, just like toothpaste and cornflakes. I'm going to be absolutely honest with you and tell you right now that if I am elected, I'm going to be the BEST GOVERNOR MONEY CAN BUY!"*

I also said that 'every form of business, government, services and most entertainment is planned to benefit the 'day' people, and "if I'm elected I would consider having legislative sessions held at night because most legislative business and lobbying is done unofficially at night away at Chuck's the Ranch or the Marion Hotel."

Gordon designed stationery for me 'Gracie For Governor', and an informational handout. There on the back was a 1968 photo of the whole family. I think that is the only photo of all of us together. We all looked so happy, but had to. I kept saying, "if you don't smile, we'll have to take lots of these until one turns out."

My family was amazing; they were always so helpful, especially Bill. He had always been the leader of the three kids, and he rallied Sis and Tom, Jr, to help out. They went and truly 'pounded the pavement' as well as stuffed sample ballots for the Democratic candidates. This was a machine happening, on weekends or evenings leading up to the election, campaign managers or party leaders would schedule a time/place to stuff ballots. Candidates would get their campaign literature to location, then people set up banquet tables with all the literature in stacks. You'd grab a ballot, walk around table and insert the brochures, someone at the end of the line would staple ballot together and pack ballots in boxes.

I didn't stop working at the Roaring 20's Room either. And I'm glad I didn't, because slated on the bill was none other than Duke Ellington and his band. I am the luckiest woman in the world, because he chose not to come right in and play with his band, no. They began to play and there was no Duke. Now, this didn't happen –ever, as he was always the showman who ruled his room. So the band started the second song and he grabbed my hand and we danced through the audience. There I was, dancing with the great Duke Ellington – at his suggestion! I could have danced all night, and when I got home, I did in my dreams.

Because I was a member of the Eastern Star and Washington Press Women's Association, it opened a lot of doors. Many people thought when I began that it was a publicity stunt. But after awhile I think Gordon and I showed them differently. Sure, I wanted and needed the publicity, but I also wanted to change the way things were being done. I studied some of the bills passed recently and what our President was saying, and I started getting really mad. Our wonderful President Nixon was the one who turned the juice on for me because of something he said about the nerve gas coming to Hermiston. I just piped up and said, "If it's so valuable and safe, why doesn't the government store it at President Nixon's California White

House?" I have always felt that nerve gas should be destroyed, and that chemical weapons stocks are morally wrong. 'Look, we pride our state on being green – why do they insist on turning the beautiful State of Oregon into a dump?'

I went to every town I could, big or small, it didn't matter. And before you knew it, even the press took me seriously. One said, "she's running a campaign fit to be Governor." I went everywhere I could, shaking hands, giving speeches and listening to people. In Albany and elsewhere, I had police escorts greet and take me to where I was to speak.

And being quoted? I thought I was making sure that no stone was left unturned.

On schooling: "I never let schooling stand in my way of an education."
On Nixon/Agnew: "I think Agnew is a brilliant man – he may prove smarter than Richard."
On Vietnam: "It's bad, and I don't blame the kids for not wanting to go. We have spent enough money to buy the country – why not? That might be the best approach." On money, "There is a big difference between having no money and having a little money, but that there is little difference between having a little money and a lot of money."

And I also stated that "am deeply concerned with the problems of our state's Senior Citizens, and the inadequacy of our present Old-age Assistance Program." And, "I am in favor of more recreational facilities toward the development of healthier minds and bodies of our increasing youth population," but, "I am against the discrimination of woman socially, economically and age-wise."

True to Gordon's word, my slogans were being used and the press ate them up. Such as, 'I've had my eye on [Governor] Tom McCall's seat for a long time.' or 'Gracie Hansen For Governor - The Best Governor Money Can Buy.' And, I will say this is truly one I believe in, "I feel I'm as qualified as any other of the comedians who are running for public office." There was something else I said that people laughed at, but I think is so true, "Everyone in Oregon is entitled to and should have three things-something to work at, something to love and something to hope for."

Thank goodness Gordon was handling the press. The State of Oregon gave me a book entitled, Candidates Daily Newspaper Hand Book – it had a donkey and an elephant on the cover, each draped with the American flag. There was too much information inside on who to send things to, when they were to be sent – if I had done that task, that alone would have made me quit.

All through the campaign I wanted it to be different. Using my 'apple' from the days of the World's Fair was that one way to be different – it certainly caught a lot of attention.

At home, an assembly line was set up at the dining room table. There were, Gracie for Governor buttons in piles just waiting for everyone to put a tiny little rhinestones, which were my signature. And, it just wasn't just the campaign buttons, even the bumper stickers and paper strips for banners had to have the tiny little rhinestones put on them. I tell, you we went through a lot of glue, rhinestones and hours. And I think we all believed it was going to pay off.

On election night, Gordon and I headed down to the Hoyt to hear election returns. Since it would be a long night, I told the kids and Tom to stay home and 'wait it out in front of the television set. If it looked like I was going to win, come down and let's celebrate; if not, just go to bed, there's school in the morning.' On the way down the first returns were coming in. Gordon turned the radio to KLIQ "from inside the Hoyt" and we heard, "This may be something historic, now people these are early returns, but at this moment Gracie Hansen is a head with of Bob Straub." I grabbed the dial and turned it off, "Now what do we do if we win?"

But I didn't. I put up a good fight. The primary went to Bob Straub to face off with the incumbent Tom McCall. The great news, though, was that out of eight on the primary ticket, I came in third with about 25,000 votes.

It was no surprise when it came to the general election that Tom McCall won reelection. He was very popular and a very sweet man as well. On election night, Gordon, Tom and I were invited up to his suite to watch the election returns with him and his wife.
When he went down to make his acceptance speech, he made sure I was right there. When a photographer snapped a photo, Tom asked if he could have a copy. Within no time one appeared, Tom McCall kissing me on the cheek. Then he wrote on the bottom right side, 'To Gracie – the best governor any money can buy. Fondly Tom McCall.' Like I said, I would have

been a Republican... (But, I'm too poor and I'm also too liberal to be a Republican)

What was I to do next? My heath really was giving me problems and I started gaining weight, thanks to the diabetes. So, I quit the Roaring 20's Room. I told Harvey it was because I needed some rest, but it was more than that. I didn't feel like it was *Gracie Hansen's Roaring 20's Room* – it needed to be someone else's. Besides, I had to get going on the publication of the Horoscope for Swingers. Fred Bay Company agreed to publish it, and I started seeking out press to sell it. I thought it would be a good idea to go to the National Enquirer. They didn't seem to have any problems with what they wrote about. They sold items all the time off their back cover, you built an ad, and included a form at the bottom to be mailed in. I had already arranged to sell it in the Oregonian - they seemed more than pleased to receive my money - but I got a rejection letter from the National Enquirer. They deemed that my book was not appropriate for their family publication. I <u>had</u> to tell the kids. We all couldn't believe that this rag was above selling an innocent book. From then on we didn't call it a 'rag', we called it a 'proper family mag'.

I mean really, all the ad said was, "You too could be swinging on the wrong star. Find out for sure in Gracie Hansen's New Book: Horoscope For Swingers." Yes, I agree, too racy.

I tried very hard to tell people what the book was about: 'Not for Prudes, Not for children; Not for those whose wing is broken and if you wanted to have it mail-ordered, I made sure that the book was sent to the house discreetly – in a plain wrapper'.

I pushed the book wherever I went. In December I went to Seattle to attend the Washington Press Women's luncheon – I'm a member. Someone walked up to me and asked what I was doing with my life lately. I told them about the book and they asked if I had brought a copy. I said, "Well, actually I was going to bring everyone a copy, but when my business manager found out I was going to do that, he said it would mean more to me if I had them buy a copy. So, I just brought up order forms." I want to tell people about the Zodiac. Many people are scared of it. "In ancient times the Zodiac was called the circle of life, with each sign making up a part of the circle. And you should look on your sign-your part of life-rather like an onion. You may cry a little when you peel it, but it sure spices things up later on! And doll, don't be afraid that your life will end – be afraid that it will never begin."

I also got a gig on a local morning talk show with Kirby Brumfield on KATU – Channel 2, the ABC station in Portland. I was the 'Horoscope Lady'; I was to tell people what was in store for their Zodiac sign. You'd look in the television listings and it would say, 'Gracie Hansen gives her weekly horoscope reading.' It was a great tie-in to my book, but the station management didn't feel that it fit the station's overall philosophy and I was let go soon after. What, were they owned by the same company as the National Enquirer?

I needed a break from all the wigs so I went into Vidal Sassoon Salon on a trip to Los Angeles and got this style that would look great and be perfect for the little natural hair I had. It was called Windswept. Well, I felt windswept when they were finished and showed me this hairstyle that I normally got when I was caught in the Portland rain and wind, as well as the feeling I got when I had to give the stylist the $70.00, not including the tip! To me, a good natural wig made from Oriental hair is the right recipe for me. They can be made, styled and look great. and all I have to do is put on a wig cap, some makeup and a few pieces of jewelry and I am done.

Again I headed to the hospital. This time for artery surgery. Tom called me and said, "the Home Magazine wants to do an article on the 'man behind the woman'. Is that okay?"

The article turned out great. It was entitled, *The Man in Gracie Hansen's life*. I think this was the first and only interview Tom ever did, he was a very private person. In it, he spilled the beans about my surgery, 'he is awaiting Gracie's surgery recovery so that they can dance together again.'

On my road to recovery, I spoke at the NW Horticultural Congress in the Spruce Room at the Memorial Coliseum. I don't think they believed they were going to get someone telling them how to plant roses.

Things really slowed down for me after I left the Hoyt. They had to, my health and all the wear and tear on my body from the years of running was catching up with me. But the things that did come my way, they came at the right time.

I was invited to Seattle for the dedication of the Gracie Hansen's Community Center. I found out later, it wasn't going to be in Seattle, but Ravensdale. Where in the hell is Ravensdale? A long way from Seattle.

This small town, smaller than Morton, is located way up in the mountains east of Seattle. You see, since the Paradise Pavilion wasn't designed to be a permanent structure (being of slab concrete), it was taken apart, stored, and now the City Commissioners of King County had found a use for it. I took Sis with me for the dedication. We flew up to Seattle, but I decided it would be best if she didn't have to drive all the way out to

Ravensdale, so she stayed with my dear friend Trig (who had moved to Seattle from Morton).

What a set of mixed emotions. The plot of land was beautiful, and the use was more than I could have asked for – but in Ravensdale? As I stood, hearing honors being bestowed on me, I kept thinking, in twenty-five years will anyone know that this ,building housed topless women and me?

You know, even though they are not your biological children, there are days you want to still strangle their necks. I heard some yelling coming from upstairs between Bill and Sis. Now, they were always at it, and then you'd hear laughter, then soon it was forgotten. But this time, doors slammed so hard the house shook. I made my way up to Sis's room, and after she let me in, I could see she was extremely upset. "What did Bill do this time?"

She sat on the bed and said, "he's ...never mind."

Without much more, I then went to Bill's. He looked like this little scared child. "Now, I know you didn't break anything or you would have told me. And I know you don't need to tell me anything, but you've made your sister a very angry young lady. So?" Now both being Leos doesn't help the situation, so I stared him down, "It won't leave this room and I won't tell your dad."

I saw a beautiful young man become a very scared little boy, "I'm gay."

I wasn't surprised. I had heard from some that they had seen Bill at some establishments that catered to gays. "And you know this?'

"Yep."

"As I promised, your dad will never know."

I never did tell Tom, he wouldn't have liked it one bit. Me? Look what I have done in my life, and I was to judge anyone else? Tom did find out later, and what I saw was that Tom Jr. became Tom's son, and Bill was left to be the middle child without a dad. I'm not saying Tom didn't love Bill, but like some parents when it came to being gay, it's hard to accept. Within a month, Bill graduated from high school and then moved to Hawaii. It would be awhile before we would see him, and that would be later in San Francisco when he invited Sis, Tom and me to come down and visit him and his friend Gary. Then, over the following years, Bill and Tom grew close again, had a lot of fun together, and I think found a genuine love between each other. I'm glad I have a gay child – it makes our family more blended, if you get my drift.

Now for a career move that I never saw happening. I was asked to be in *La Rondine* (the Swallow) by Puccini. Those who know me, well they know that the songs of Sophie Tucker are more my style. But, guess what, I played the Nightclub Entertainer for the Portland Opera's opening show. Dressed in dazzlingly bedecked green satin bloomers (they kept falling to my ankles) hiding my green and white striped stockings (that also kept falling down), and with the yellow clown blouse with green ruffles around my neck and wrists – I am told that the costume was copied from the painting by Toulouse-Loutrec entitled, 'La Clownessa." Now, wasn't my role the 'Nightclub Entertainer?' Well, I was distinctly warned not to sing, not even to open my mouth except to utter two words as I walked swaggeringly around the stage, "aha" and again, "aha". But I didn't care – I was doing an opera! I put my heart into it, one hand on the back of my head, and the other akimbo on my hip, I flung myself a whirling motion around the stage – thinking only of the other greats like Caruso and Maria Callas. At curtain call, as I stood there in the chorus, I am positive I heard one BRAVO for me.

Well, the whole experience was truly educational and exciting. It was the first time I ever got my own dresser – someone who powdered my nose and hung everything up neatly. And then...nine days later I was in *The Song of Norway*.

'Never step on people on the way up, because you might need them when you are stepping down.' Truer words were never spoken. I got a call from John Hillsbury – yes, the original choreographer from the early days at the Hoyt. He asked if I'd like to be part of a show he was staging. I could hardly contain myself, "John, are you sure you want me?"

His reply, "Only you."

He was doing a benefit for the Portland Children's Center for two days only, and they were doing *The Song of Norway* an opera by Grieg. Now, I don't think Grieg would ever have imagined me singing one of his songs – neither would I! But, with a slight nudge, I said yes, and with John's help (god bless him), I went on stage with the United First Methodist Youth and Children's Choir (those Methodist always come back into my life, don't they?) the Portland Chamber Orchestra, and a cast of what seemed like a thousand. What a blast. A lot of work, but a lot of fun. It was also great reconnecting with someone from my first days in Portland. John was gracious and helped me so much.

The fun part was that I was writing for the Community Press at the time and got to tell the world about my exploits at the opera – I think if I hadn't, no one would have believed it.

And with two operas under my belt, 'retirement' from the opera stage was in order. Okay, honestly, after *La Rondine* and *The Song of Norway*, no one ever asked me again.

Over the past year, I went down to Los Angeles to see if I could make something happen with my career. What career? I know, but I've been entertaining people more of my life than anything else, so I thought I'd see if the entertainment capitol of the world would open its doors. This was to be a blessing and a curse. First, I learned that you have to have an agent – and not just any agent, an agent who will believe in you and work for you.

I received a call saying that there was a 'perfect' part for me in a nationally televised show entitled *Arnie.* It was in its second year and had a big lead-in show – *The Mary Tyler Moore Show.* "This would be great exposure and the perfect part." I didn't even ask to see the script, I just wanted to know if my name would be mentioned anywhere. "Well, you won't be Gracie in the episode, but you will receive credit, which is a very big start." Tom, Gordon and I flew to LA for filming. I wanted to impress everyone, so I wore my normal jewelry and a better-than- average wig. When I walked on set and met the director, he said, "we'll get you into wardrobe and hair; you can't wear all that for this shoot. I was a bit taken back and said, "but how will people in Portland know who I am?" He smiled and said, 'I don't think they will have any trouble."

The shoot was fun, the cast was wonderful (I met Charles Nelson Reilly, amongst others) and yes, I got a credit with my name. The episode was entitled, *Wilson Tastes Good Like a Candidate Should*. Herschel Bernardi was Arnie and I was the campaign lady – that was my name: 'the campaign lady'. It aired on Saturday February 26, 1972. I felt like 1972 was going to be a very good year. The press went out, 'Century 21 Proprietor: National TV Debut': Guileless Gracie Hansen....will make her national TV debut this Saturday/26 on CBS. Effervescent Gracie,
Oregon's last Democratic gubernatorial candidate, will appear as campaign worker with star Herschel Bernardi.

After doing that one episode of *Arnie*, I was told by my agent that there 'may be some work' for me on television. So we stayed in Los Angeles a couple extra days. What seemed like a big possibility was a new detective series based on the A. A. Fair books which characters were named Bertha Cool and Donald Lam. A meeting was set up with Charles B. Fitzsimmons a producer/writer and actor in the midst of producing the hit show *Nanny and the Professor*. What I didn't know was that he also was the brother of Maureen O'Hara! At our initial meeting Charles said, "I was hoping for a big gal." I choked. This was the first time in my whole life that they (the producers) said that I wasn't fat enough! He was kind, polite and told me that this was just in the talking stage. "You see a pilot was shot in 1958 called *Cool and Lam* but never became a series. It was loosely based on the book *Turn On The Heat*." He went on to say that Bertha Cool is described as overweight and uncaring about her weight, and that Donald Lam estimates that a 'cool' 220! She does lose weight through the books and slims down to about 165. She is also described as a woman with white hair and "greedy piggish eyes". In all books she is also described as extremely avaricious and miserly, and her favorite statement is 'Fry me for an oyster!'

Some of this was me, and a lot of it wasn't. But it was a lead in a prime-time show.

Charles continued, "Bertha hires Donald Lam, a small (5' 6" tall/125 pounds) and extremely ingenious disbarred lawyer who later becomes a full partner in her business. There are enough books to provide several years of material – 29 books in all." And that's how our meeting ended – he handed me several books by Erle Stanley Garner books, thanked me and told me to go read them.

Later that evening we got a call to come over to Charles' house. I was deep in the first book, but when someone who can change your life calls, you run. When we got there, nothing had changed; oh, Charles was a little bit more relaxed, and I kept hearing Gordon say all the way over to the house, "this is a second look- he wants to see you away from the office. This could be very good or very bad." So, in my head I was listening to Gordon while my heart was falling for Bertha, and trying to keep my focus on Charles. After small .talk and dinner he gave me an old LP- 78 and told me that this was the 'type of music the show invokes' – the music was John Barrymore! This was the Hollywood I had heard about – the wine, the dine, the gifts, and all I wanted was for him to say, "and you're hired'. But, he didn't. What he did was thank us all again, told us to have a safe journey home, and said goodnight. I held onto the LP all the way to the hotel, and when we got back to Portland, it went right on the fireplace mantle. Do you know who A. A. Fair really was? His real name was Erle Stanley Gardner and he wrote all the Perry Mason books – this could be something.

Now, I'm not into numerology but my 'career' took off in 1961 with Century 21, and now in 1971 I am working at 20th Century Fox in another career highlight. Would I have to wait another 10 years for anything else to happen? But, please put me in a better outfit – I looked old and frumpy – but I guess that's what you do, right? Do what the role calls for and get your name credited.

While in Los Angeles I noticed that my legs, if I stood or sat for very long, hurt. So, when we got back home, I went to the doctor. "Gracie, you need surgery as you have what appears to be blocked arteries." I couldn't stand the pain, so I told him to make it as soon as possible. When word got out that I was going to have surgery, all my dear friends started donating blood. I couldn't believe they would be so generous – but I didn't realize that I would need all those pints! But, what I didn't like was that I was having basically the same surgery as I had before. This, to me, was not a good sign. I went to OHSU for surgery to try to unblock blockages in arteries in both my legs. I was told that the surgery was performed on my right leg first. But, after surgery the leg started hemorrhaging and I was rushed back into surgery to have another operation. After I came to, the doctor told me what had happened and that they only did the right leg and that they would have to go back in to do the left. He had scheduled surgery for April 8th and said that I'd be up on my feet in no time. When someone tells you that, ask the next question – 'will I be as good as new?'

While I was having surgery, a letter lay waiting to be opened. It was from William Fowler of 20th Century Fox. He was responsible for TV Publicity. Tom mentioned to me that Bill (as I got to call him) was the first reporter on the scene at the infamous Black Dahlia murders – he was somebody.
I opened the letter when I got home and began recuperating, why was it letting me down now?

Dear Gracie:
What happened to you? Did you drop into the Black Hole of Calcutta! Haven't heard from you.

Enclosed please find copies of four stories I wrote for the Oregonian, Journal, Seattle Times and the Post-Intelligencer re: your upcoming stint on the "Arnie" episode February 26. (Incidentally, the script was taken from an anecdote from my book, YOUNG MAN FROM DENVER – hope you've found time to read it). I'm planting your story locally here with the Times and the Herald & Express, also with the wire services (AP & UPI). Also enclosed is a Xerox copy of the Los Angles Press Club newspaper telling of Rex Henson's appearance there with his gang. You're having a cue of stars that will attend along with many local critics. Rex asked me to say "hello" and asked what you want him to do about writing that material for you.

Again, are you making that tape and/or film so I can get it to LAUGH IN for you?

Send my best along to Gordon,
Warm regards from
Will Fowler

I cried and cried and cried. There was an open door and my body said, 'nah, don't go in.'
And I got strong enough to go right back in the hospital in April for my left leg. Fortunately, it wasn't as bad a surgery – but stil,l I wasn't ready for Hollywood, and after a few seconds, Hollywood truly does forget even a flicker of a rising star.

What I didn't realize until I got this next call that it had actually been 10 years since the World's Fair had taken place. 10 YEARS! Where had it gone? The 10th Anniversary organization committee stated, "Gracie you were always classy, top notch and we want you to be our 'kick-off girl'." I asked exactly what a 'kick-off girl' meant to them., They said, there would be a 10' birthday cake was being built, and that I would jump out of it. I get the 10' for 10 years, funny, but me coming out of a cake like that? Hell, why not! This was to 'kick off' a 10 day celebration (these 10s are killing me) from April 21-30 at the Seattle Center.

So, I went up and was part of the celebration. It was fun. And, yes, there was that 10' tall cake, with balloons everywhere, and, me as the 'topper'. I wore this great outfit, black jeweled top with silver leggings and silver boots. When I did 'come out of the cake' I got the response that I had hoped for. "Look out, Seattle, Gracie's back!"
The night before, a party was held at the Golden Lion of the Olympic Hotel. With Tubby Clark at the piano, I sang, talked, told jokes and just reminisced about the World's Fair days. When an article came out in the Seattle Post-Intelligencer the next day, they called me the 'Queen of the Fair'...the reigning queen of the Seattle World's Fair....they said I was 'a symphony of rhinestones, feathers and laughter.' Where was that quote back in '62?

During my chat I said something that has stayed with me all my years from Morton until now. "I had two things going for me, ignorance and confidence. If you are too dumb to know things can't be done, then you do them." Right?

Now, I am one to just say what I think, and sometimes say things out of turn. You are going to say, 'really Gracie?' So, when the press asked me what I was up to next, I just blurted out, 'Soon I will have a 'minor starring role' in a motion picture with Raquel Welch. It's a roller-derby story, *The Kansas City Bomber*. Raquel what's-her-name is very worried about the competition!' Was it true? Well, when filming started at the Expo Center, I was there as an extra for about a day. I don't think they used my footage, but I wasn't going to be a liar, so at least I 'put in my days' work'.

The press followed me over to where Building 90 – The Paradise Pavilion had stood. Now it was just a corner lot with a mound of dirt. I said, without really thinking, but I meant it with all my heart, "That's the Gracie Hansen Memorial Park- someday I'm going to plant a marker there." I haven't yet, but someday is still just around the corner.

Later on in September I received a certificate in the mail, (hadn't I received one 10 years ago?) saying "Seattle Center Salutes GRACIE HANSEN". I <u>had</u> made a difference at the Fair, hadn't I?

Right after we got home, I got a phone call. Mom's sister Jo had just died. Mom didn't want to tell me how, but after I persisted, she explained. 'Grace, Jo had diabetes. This was bad. She had what is known as a 'brittle'; she had to have both her legs removed. And sweetie, I wanted to tell you weeks ago, but I couldn't.'
'Are you telling me Aunt Jo died earlier this month?'
'Yes, but so much was going on with you.'
She couldn't say it, could she? I was in the hospital having my left leg worked on about the same time Aunt Jo died.

I couldn't sit around after hearing that. Yes, my legs hurt, but my heart hurt worse, so I became involved with Loaves and Fishes on 52nd and Woodstock to serve the needy in any capacity. If I was asked to speak, do guest honors and emcee various functions at the Rotary Club, the Jaycees, The Elks, even the Junior League (was I now 'acceptable'?) I did it. I started taking writing and painting classes; signed up for workshops that focused on self-awareness as well as healing oneself. One thing I tried was hypnosis for weight control. I have always battled the 'bulge problem' since I was a child. Look at the photos, you'll see – there probably was not a photo that doesn't show some girth around my waistline. The problem with eating is that you have to eat to live – it's pretty important.

I was so restless that I thought it might be a good idea for me to run for public office again. I believed the old adage, 'if you don't succeed...' So I ran for State Representative against Gladys McCoy and a young man named Earl Blumenauer. I bet you are going to ask what my platforms were, right? Well, what do you think about: "The big thing in my campaign is property tax relief. Everybody needs it – including me!" (it's still true today) and I wanted to get a break for 'night people' like myself. The night people are being discriminated against. There are thousands and thousands of us. But the whole world is geared for day people." (nobody who didn't work nights got that one.) I didn't push or work as hard at it, because once I realized that Gladys was everyone's favorite – how hard can you push? She was going to win. I was still actively involved in the Democratic party and became a delegate to the National Party Convention for the Third Congressional District.

Then one day, I got a phone call from Esther, she had received notice that Roderick her son was missing in action, MIA – in Vietnam. We both cried that day, a lot. Esther said, 'they always say, you never want to bury your young...but Gracie, I don't know if he will ever be buried.' We cried some more. Then I had to call Sambo – Roderick and Sambo were like glue in Morton and now the glue wasn't there anymore.

My health just wasn't cooperating with me. I guess age had something to do with it? But, you don't think age is that much of a factor until you get old – then watch out! I had heard about psychic surgeries that 'will heal your body, mind and soul'. Tom was skeptical, I was hopeful, so we watched movies, read testimonies – it seemed that those who did it, they were cured. Cured was a good word for me. I told Gordon our plans and he agreed to go with us, so off we went to 'try it out', all the way to the Philippines. We flew all the way to Baguio City for the psychic surgery. It turned out to be a phony deal. Those 'surgeons' were actually palming chicken guts or some other junk and telling you that they were taking out tumors and growths.

I didn't know how bad it was at the Hoyt. Johanna had taken over the management of the hotel, was doing 'me' on stage, and that's when Rene' quit and went back to Las Vegas. Roc had moved in with Walter, who had just won the title of "Imperial Court Empress" and was crowned Darcelle. They had been turning the Dumas tavern into a club that did only drag, all the time, Darcelle XV. It was a smash, but three blocks away, the Hoyt was dying. The ironic twist to life? When Rene' left, Jack

Card was hired to be the new director/choreographer. Yes, the same Jack Card who in 1961 I had talked to about working with me at the World's Fair. The same Jack Card that sued me and got over $27,000 because I used his name and promoted him as my director/ choreographer at the World's Fair.

Now, Jack was running things at the Roaring 20's Room. He had brought down from Canada a wonderful singer by the name of Richard Hurst, who he thought would be a draw. And he insisted that the costumes that had been used weren't up to the caliber of his stage show and talked Harvey into spending $20,000 on new costumes! The show was called *What A Night.* There were 13 dancers and Le Roy Anderson as the band leader. It played Tuesday through Friday, twice a night and three times on Saturday. For awhile the show sold, but maybe it was that Harvey didn't take checks or credit cards, which was getting to be a big thing then, or that people still had to wear dresses, ties and jackets, but for whatever reason, things started going downhill.

One night, in early August Gordon and a date went down to see the new show that Jack Card had staged at the Hoyt. He told me later that his conversation with Harvey wasn't very good, "Looks like things aren't the way they used to be." Harvey replied, "No, but it's summer, and things have always been a bit slow around this time." But looking around the 500 seat room and seeing that he and his date were the only ones there for the 10 pm show Gordon said, "Harvey, if you would see fit, I'd like to buy this place, lock, stock, and barrel - let's say for $250,000." Harvey smiled, "Thank you, but that won't be necessary, things will pick up soon." A couple days later the Hoyt closed (August

4th) and all of those who were working or loyal to Harvey were asked to leave the building and the doors were sealed.

I have this plaque hanging on the door handle at the back door, it has a little tramp resting by a rock with his knapsack. The caption reads, "If you're so damn smart...why ain't you rich?" The Hoyt closing reminds me of that saying. I know you can't go back and do a 'would've, should've, could've', and if what Gordon told me was true, the old man was like the captain of a sinking ship: or he was going to go down with it and with honor. Since the possibility of obtaining the Hoyt was out of the question, Gordon and I talked during that time about trying to find another space to open. Gordon thought that we should pull in some investors and find a nice space in downtown. We looked at the space which is now Jake's — it had a wonderful bar area, but not much of a back room to do shows. We looked at others, like the building that housed the old 'Castaways' restaurant/ lounge/nightclub. But, with my health and no buildings to really believe in, we said to each other, maybe it isn't time. Too bad, it never would be.

The Hoyt sat silent until early November. That's when Harvey put a huge full-page ad in the Oregonian and declaring that an auction was to be held. And it was going to be big!

Held on November 18th, 19th, 20th. (now, no numerology stuff again, but the second year of the Morton Follies were held on November 18th and 19th.) Gordon and I had to go. When we walked in, we were handed a large, beautifully printed almost twenty page booklet outlining all the items for auction. Each day had specific items listed for sale. It wasn't until the final day when the Fotoplayer, the 2,500 miniature liquor bottles, the Rolls Royce, chastity belt and Castro were to be sold.

Flipping through the booklet I noticed a letter of introduction by Harvey, it read, 'For the past 15 years I have been actively collecting the art objects listed in this catalogue. In my searches I have traveled up and down the Pacific Coast, into Canada, and into some foreign countries. Each item was selected because it appealed to me personally. I am not happy about disposing of these treasures but, unfortunately, it is necessary for me to do so at this time. I doubt if you will ever have another opportunity to purchase art treasures from a collection as large as the one I have accumulated over the years. Thank you for attending, and I hope you find many things you like.' After reading that, I felt faint.

We walked around and looked at a place which once was majestic, now a disaster. My home for almost six years was being dismantled. The stain glass panels on the outside of my room were leaning up against the wall in the lobby, the French chandeliers that once hung in the Roaring 20's room seemed to be tossed against the wall. I remember telling somebody from the press, "We got those stained glass windows from a church that was being demolished. We thought we cut out all the religious figures, but a priest the other night said that the one with wings is the Holy Ghost. Hell, we thought it was a seagull."

My heart ached at what my eyes saw. The once grand showcase was now just a dismantled looking warehouse with objects to be bought at the cheapest price possible.

I couldn't believe the pleasure people were having buying items for next nothing.

I didn't get anything. My heart wasn't into it. I wanted to go the final day, but Gordon had to leave town and Tom didn't want to go – so I sat looking at the booklet. There will never be another grand dame such as the Hoyt Hotel. Why did this have to happen? Why did it have to be sold? What would become of the Hoyt? God forbid it might even be demolished.

Harvey, Harvey, Harvey.

What did come my way was a movie part. No, not with Raquel Welch, but in a movie that was going to be produced locally by a young man named Tom Moyer, Jr. His father was a bigwig in the ownership of cinemas in the area. Tom, Jr. hired all local: Jim Bosley, a local television personality; Mark Allen, a local theatre producer; Alan Hirsh, a radio talk show host. It was to be Tom, Jr.'s first movie as a director/producer and writer. Tom asked if I was worried about one man wearing so many hats, and I just looked at him and said, 'if a woman can do it, so can a man.' It was shot with a tiny budget. But the premiere – it was huge! Must have been bigger than the whole movie budget, Broadway was shut down, there was a marching band, a total of 3,000 people were invited. Sis and Bill dressed up to the nines and went with Tom and me. I was in a movie, it didn't matter how good or bad, but I was doing what any good person does with ambition, add another credit to their resume'.

What happened to the movie after the Portland premiere? Well, rumor has it that Tom, Jr. didn't have enough financing and even though it was to have a second premiere in Washington, DC, nothing came of it.

Like I have always said, you get a high, you'll get a low. "Gracie, this is George. Gracie, it's mom..."

He couldn't speak after that. We both just sat on the phone and cried.

My Momma died of a heart attack on January 11th.
Momma, Momma, Momma. I cannot tell you how hard it was hearing about her dying. At the age of 69, her heart didn't want to work anymore. And mine? It beat, but it really hurt.

I closed my eyes and thought of her scent – it wasn't roses anymore, but White Shoulders.

Tom and I went up for her funeral, everyone was there. It was like a family reunion and I tried to celebrate her life. What helped was seeing relatives who I hadn't seen forever, like Mom's brother Tony and his Cherokee wife from Oklahoma.

On the way home I told Tom that I needed to understand about death. Mom and Dad were raised Catholics but never raised us in that faith, and then turned around and had us go and attend a church that taught Christian doctrine. But I kept saying, and I still do, it didn't answer questions about death. I know it is going to happen, it does happen and will happen.

Almost two months to the day later, Uncle Tony died. Hadn't I just seen him at Mom's funeral? I was told that he collapsed at home of heart failure and died instantly. What is scaring me the most? I figured out that all three of the siblings, Mom, Jo and Tony, all died within ten months of each other and that death comes in threes. We were done, right? Nope, then Mike Fairhart died. I didn't go to Morton, I couldn't.

While at Momma's funeral, Carl asked me to come over and spend some time in Spokane. It's not exactly a destination city of my choice, but when your baby brother asks you nicely, then you go. And we went. It is truly a beautiful city, such as it is. But, after talking to Carl and his wife Ollie, I began to realize that another World's Fair was going to take place. It was going to be 'World's Expo '74' which was billed as the Spokane World's Exposition – the Environmental World's Fair. That title was bigger than the fair site itself. I started, just slightly to get excited when I heard they were going to reserve a whole block of the park for an entertainment area. I thought...maybe? And then I laughed, NO! They banned my *Horoscope for Swingers* up here...they'd close me down in no time. But while visiting, KGW's affiliate KREM (really, cream?) asked me to come on the air. Well, I put on some feathers, did an interview, and then strolled around town, if nothing more than to shake up the natives. God, did I have fun.

But coming back to Portland put a damper on the fun we had in Spokane, and the rest of 1973 and some of '74 was, and still is a blur. I did help promote Gordon's race horses down in Salem and out at Portland Meadows, but my heart. I had lost people who were close to me and I couldn't find answers. All the years in Morton, and the death that happened there, all the joyous years in Seattle and Portland, and now...

Being confused, Tom agreed, to go with me and interview people who were facing death, go to mortuaries and ask questions, we even went so far as attend several séances. It was then that I decided that a box wasn't for me: 'burn me and spread me out into the desert – I want to be warm for eternity.'

I did try my best to help the wonderful Forchuk brothers when they opened The Organ Grinder on SE 82nd in Portland. At the beginning it was a huge hit, with families especially. It was being touted as being as the best pizza parlor anywhere with a fully- functioning theatre pipe organ. Being Italian, I thought sure, I'll give it a whirl, but it just wasn't what I wanted. Adults were there for the kids, the kids were there to hear the organ and eat loads of pizzas. I told Dennis Hedberg (who was also part owner), "you know Italians like more than pizza!"

And he replied, "yes, but I'm not seeing a lot of Italians eating here."

Being tired of being tired, one day I sat down in the living room and looked around. And when you are all alone, what you see is 'things' – not my life. When we first bought the house and had everything redone, I also had a whole wall dedicated to photos – 'a wall of memories' – photos of me and Johnny Carson, the girls from Paradise and the Hoyt – those still gave me comfort. No, it was all the other 'things' that I needed to take charge of – they seemed to be ruling me and owning me and not the other way around. So, in August, I began taking charge and by September held my first-ever garage sale. Not what I expected, as people wanted to see the inside of the house and meet me rather than to buy things. So, they got to see the inside of my home, they got to meet me, and they took my 'things' with them when they left. It was fun, exhausting and not financially rewarding.

In one of the boxes I found some of the jokes that I had compiled. Now, normally the good ones were put in a filing cabinet but these, I wonder if they were not right, not good or? 'Summer clothes—summer paid for and so-mer not.' 'You're wondering why I'm dressed like this---no excuse---but there're a lot of reasons.' 'Do you want me to explain why I'm here? 'cause I know you're gonna wonder sooner or later.' And this one, 'I use organic makeup, absolutely no preservative-it's made out of banana oil, strawberry crème & cucumber paste. I put it on when I went to bed and when I woke up my face had spoiled!' Maybe that's why they are in this box.

Oh, the real prize was laying at the bottom of one box. A bunch of green stamps. I love green stamps....I horde green stamps – oh god, look, I have seven whole books – I think it took me seven whole years to collect these things too!

What I was not expecting was for Jeanette to call and tell me that George Sr. had died. "Grace, Daddy was 84 and lived a good life."
All I could say, "why couldn't he have lived a good life until he was 85?"

Another funeral; another family gathering; another drive up and down the I-5 and another face with a word that I was beginning to wish didn't exist: death.

One morning I decided I hadn't done enough for Mom or George when they were alive. They didn't need money, as they had enough for them; and they didn't need us kids, for when they wanted us they made sure we were told. And I do think Mom and I resolved a lot of our issues over the years. And George? The best second father any girl would ever want. However, I felt like, even though my health was rocky and, well, my mental state wasn't that great, I had to go and help not just at Loaves and Fishes, but also at Volunteers of America. A press person asked me why I donated my time and energy, and I said, "I'm working off a guilt complex. I feel guilty for all the things I didn't do for my parents when they were alive." And volunteering without a being 'on stage' did help.

For so many years I'd try and go back to where I was in Morton - when I would close the curtains and hide from the world. No, this time I was facing the world and was going to win the fight.

I did something I said I would never do – go to a high-school class reunion. What you notice – we all have changed. Some women were prettier, some not so much, and the ones that changed the most? THE MEN. Why? But, there I am in the class photo, *Class of 1940*. We all agreed the difference between 'she's good-looking" and 'she's looking good' is approximately twenty years and twenty pounds.

On my off-hours I was Gracie the housewife, and was around if Sis needed help. She was the last kid in school, she started being a typical high-school girl. The subject she was studying started with a B and ended in an S and had four letters – boys. She was pretty and I told Tom, "this could be trouble." But, to be honest, trouble wasn't her middle name while she was in school. Was I worried that what I had done, she would do? I just hope not.

The reading of George's will was held, stating that George, Jr., should have the house. Jeanette thought it would be good if we could go through Mom and George Sr.'s stuff and see if we'd want something, before George moved in. Hadn't we all tried to clean the house out earlier? The reading got all the kids Jeanette, Carl, George, me together for the first time without a death or crisis in what seemed like forever. The will stated that there were still two sets of old apartments and in Longview that would be divided between the four of us. It was quickly agreed that none of us were ever going to live in Longview again and so they were sold.

That got me thinking, these had been Daddy's stuff since the late 20's? Sure, Mom would have gotten them and then when she married George, it would had been theirs. Now they were ours? I told Jeanette that it felt odd having something that was my dad's. He died in 1930 and here it was 1975 – forty five years had gone by and I had driven the I-5 many times and never even thought about owning something in Longview.

Gordon called me early on February 23rd, "Have you heard about Harvey?"

"It was early and I'm not good with being up early. 'No, what happened?"

"He died in front of Joe Weston's Dolph Apartments of an apparent heart attack."

"Not again."

"What?"

"Nothing. Gordon, he was good to me – too bad he didn't sell the Hoyt to you when he could have."

When I put down the phone I didn't cry. There was a lump in my throat, but I didn't cry. I hadn't seen Harvey in a couple years, but right then I felt like I had lost a very dear friend –a dear friend indeed.

Isn't it odd, you live in a town that you can drive across in ten minutes, but you can't drive to a friend's house five minutes away?

Life is slipping away from us.

I was looking at something, that I had totally forgotten about – I was asked by the Providence Medical Center to be part of their fundraising campaign entitled, *Take A Bow*. I was asked to be part of the *Salute to Show Business*. There were so many people there from the political and business world – some were Al Jolson, Bing Crosby, Frank Sinatra, Eddie Cantor and me? Sophie Tucker! The 'fund-raiser' had eighteen scenes...longer than any show I had ever been in – never will I do that again! It was for a good cause, but once was definitely enough.

I had always said, when Sis graduates then we were going to sell the house. It actually was too much for Tom and me. I had a hard time walking up and down the stairs; when what we really needed was something small for the two of us. Even though I never walked up and down the stairs, I knew as I got older, I wouldn't even attempt, so why have a house with them anyway?

So, this was the year, 1976. Sis graduated and the house went on the market for $59,590. Signing the papers I said (and the sorry thing, it came true), "'Beige People' will probably end up buying our little piece of paradise and changing everything."

The problem is that the house didn't sell for months and months, so in early 1977, Tom and I felt like we should help an old friend who used to be the Head of Security at the Paradise Pavilion: now a Seattle City Councilman, Wayne Larkin was launching a run for Mayor of Seattle. I didn't know at the time, but almost every Council person was running, so Wayne's odds were slim. But, waiting for a house to sell or being part of a campaign – Gracie chooses the campaign! We moved up to the Magnolia section of Seattle, and when the press heard I was helping, they asked me why and I told them, to "spice up the campaign, besides, I'm an opportunist, honey, always looking for an opportunity."

Wayne told me confidentially that if he were to win, there was a possibility that I could work in his administration, and if that was the way I was going to be in politics, that was fine with me.

Why is it, when you put plans in motion, something always happens? It seemed for a while that Tom and I were two ships passing in the dark – Tom was working days, welding, and I was busy helping with Wayne's campaign. I remember this one night

I had just dolled myself up ready to go to a fund-raiser (which I seemed to be doing a lot back then, that or attending political rallies,) and I was about to leave, Tom came through the door. Now, you know when something is wrong, at least I do, and I was stopped cold in my tracks, "something happened?" He looked at me, dripping wet from the awful rain that night, and he said, "mama, almost hit a kid riding on a bike, swerved and just missed him....I came real close..., I have a problem."

That was all I needed to hear. I got the yellow pages out and found the number for AA.

Since that day my Tom has been clean and sober. He sure visited a lot of church basements, probably saw every church basement in Seattle, as that's where the meetings are generally held, but he never touched another drop after that. Thank you, AA. I cannot say enough.

As expected, Wayne didn't win. But we also couldn't get out of our lease.

Here's the ironic part about life. I've said that Tom had a drinking problem, and the only job he could find was – as a bartender. What I have learned is that some of the best bartenders don't drink. Ironic, here is a man going to AA to not drink, but he's pouring drinks for other people. What happened to me during this time? I tried to heal. If I didn't have to be on my feet, after awhile, they didn't hurt. So, it was nice not having to do practically anything. But, Seattle can be pretty dreary in the winter. Okay, downright dreary, especially if you have nothing to do.

One of the big bright spots was that the Irvington house sold. It was to close, and all of our stuff was still in it! Being in Seattle wasn't great for me, as I didn't have any way of just running down to Portland and packing things up. And I didn't want to go through a garage sale again, especially in March. So, after talking it over with Gordon, he came up with a great idea. "Make it an exclusive type of sale – one that makes people think they are getting in and getting the good stuff."

"Gordon, they ARE getting the good stuff!"

Gordon met with the people from Kitty Geddes, and she did an amazing job selling most of our stuff. Some of the stuff I thought was valuable was always moving with us, so I wasn't worried what she was going to sell – just sell it!

Here's how the ad read:

2628 NE 21 (South of Knott) Gracie Hansen sells her home!!

Red Velvet sofa and Mr. and Mrs. Chairs; Marble-top tables; large buffet; King bed, Red Velvet drapes with Austrian drape curtains; Cedar Chests; Dinette Set; Lamps; pictures; Electric Fireplace; Hollow body electric bass guitar with amp; double oven range; 'crown' sauna, French phone; lots of Candlewick glass; much more – Hoyt Hotel Memorabilia.

Since Harvey had died, some of us from the Hoyt felt like we should have a reunion to honor what we all did there and honor him as well. Being in Seattle, I did as much planning as I could over the phone, but thank goodness for Gordon and the others, it all came off without too much of a hitch.

So, on October 29th the first-ever reunion of performers from the Hoyt was held at the Elks Club. It started at 3 pm and we promised 'it would last till we run out of gas!'

It was like old times being back-stage with many of those I had shared a backstage with some twelve years earlier! What surprised me the most was Walter/Darcelle – he was all dressed up in this cowboy outfit and I said, "I didn't think you ever performed at the Hoyt."

He chuckled, "Darlin', the Hoyt was my coming out." He turned around and shook his butt! He had on butt-less chaps! And then he scooted on out to sing "I'm a Rhinestone Cowboy." Peering through the curtains I thought, 'Why would anyone wait for me if they get that now!'

I was a woman torn between two cities, actually three. Seattle was good, but nothing was happening there; Portland was where family was and Hollywood, that town was still on my mind.

When the lease was finally up in Seattle, Tom and I heartily agreed, 'Portland' it was! This was to be temporary, as I felt like I should try Los Angeles 'one more time' – our plans were to lease for six months and then head to LA around October 15th. We found this duplex in Gresham at 3347 NE 5th Court, close to Sambo, who was now married with a couple kids. He was my son, and I wanted to be close to him, if just for a while. It felt like an eternity; I wanted, no I needed to be near him. He was my Sambo, and I didn't know the man he had become and I wanted to. After serving in the military it seemed like there was a huge gap between us. Maybe, just maybe, this was one way to bridge the gap a bit?

But living in Gresham and with nothing to do, I started getting antsy. I have always said that I need a project or else I get into trouble. I sat down with Sambo and told him that I felt that I should take one more stab at Hollywood.

He looked at me and asked, "is this the next big thing?"

"No Doll," I said, "it's the last attempt. I never said that we were going to live in Gresham forever."

So, I can't get into politics but guess who did? My baby brother George! He became a Thurston County Commissioner. All I could say when he called with the news was, "good for you – I'm starting to believe politics is just for men." He kept getting elected; he whispered to me, "I think the secret is to have the name George."

Los Angeles
'If I would had listened to everyone, I'd still be a frumpy, fat, housewife from Morton – I say, "who gives a damn."'

We loaded up everything and headed for Hollywood. This was my make-or-break trip. It had been almost 6 years since I was here last, but I thought, like the song says, 'If you make it here, you'll make it anywhere.' (just don't sing the rest of it and it applies to any town). I was eager. Eager as any teenager to make it in this business. I started taking workshops and I even joined a small acting troupe, started feeling like I would make it, and even getting into some no-name productions. I was even asked to perform stand up in a club on Wilshire Blvd. Tom found a job working in a welding shop and we finally found a small apartment in North Hollywood. When people asked, 'where are you? I'd say, 'in Hollywood' and wouldn't be lying, right? Life was good. Tom and I were like kids in a candy store – laughing at stupid things, loving the important things. And the kids? Tom Jr. was in Portland, Bill, god bless him, lived in, where else, San Francisco, Sis – she ran off with a guy, and well, we haven't really seen her, and Sambo was in Gresham. They were their responsibilities – we were ours.

What do you do in LA? You shop. I, we, had been shopping all day long and I couldn't wait to get my shoes off. I always say, "Doll, wear comfortable shoes when you shop – you last longer." I told Tom earlier that my foot had been hurting but, "I'll last the day out."
He kept teasing, "are you sure it's not your legs?"

I told him, I looked over at him, "I am more than confident that I know the difference between a leg and a foot." Anyway, when I took my right shoe off I couldn't believe my eyes, my little toe was almost black – like it had exploded, it was so big.

I tried to stay calm, but my voice said otherwise, "Oh no...no...no."

Tom was putting bags away and said, "Mama, you okay?"

All I could say was, "look."

He turned around, took one look and grabbed the phone.

We got in right away to see my doc and he immediately made arrangements with a vascular surgeon in Santa Monica. Fortunately, he said it was an emergency, because we were shown right in, and when he examined my foot, he immediately took off his jacket and told the nurse to get hold of UCLA Medical Center – "we are on our way."

He drove us. On the way over, he told me that he was going to rush me into surgery to do a 'simple operation'. I told him that I had been through operations and found nothing simple about them. "Once we get to UCLA, we're going to prep you for surgery. I'm going to try to put a in Dacron tube. Gracie, your foot is dying and I'm going to try and save it."

All the time, Tom sat quietly in the back seat.

When you are filled with all kinds of pain killers that just knock you for a loop, there isn't much that you remember. All in all, I lost weeks of what I knew as life.

Doc tried his best, but my surgery wasn't healing. One of the problems-I'm allergic to penicillin. So they tried to give me stronger pain killers, but I could only take so many of those and the stronger medication is, the harder for your body to heal fast.

Then infection set in.

I was handed over to an orthopedic surgeon. My toe was gone by now, amputated. He hurried to try and save the rest of my foot.

I was transferred over to St John's in Santa Monica, and there I had a second surgery that took off my leg right below the knee. I was in and out of the hospital for surgery after surgery after surgery. The doc told Tom, "I tried to retain her knee, and I hope we have enough healthy tissue and good blood supply to allow proper healing."

The nurses were fluttering all around and I kept asking questions, but in a drug induced state, it's hard to get a word out or understand what anyone was talking about. Once I could figure out what was happening it began to sink in that I was being prepped for surgery. Again. Later, the nurse told me my response was, "gee, we've been here what seems like forever, we should had me prepped by now." She patted my hand, "yes dear, you have and this isn't the first time you've been in surgery today."

When it began to sink in that things were turning from bad to worse, Tom turned to Maureen for help. She immediately flew down from Portland. She wasn't worried as much for me, but for Tom. With already had one heart attack, she felt it wasn't necessary to have both her dad and me in the hospital.

Hours ticked by and finally the doctor came out to talk to Tom, "I think we're successful."
Thank goodness for Carl's notes, so I knew what had happened to me wasn't just an 'acting lesson':
Grace   1-213-982-3247   (California   phone   #) bad   place   -- not healing -- too well   back to hospital.
Maureen is there to take care of her -- in wheel chair --   R. leg up to knee off --
Whole leg artery plugged   6 full operations-- tried to by pass -- Little ulcers keep coming up -- lost about 30 pounds
Is this any way to lose weight?

When Tom walked into the room I said, "Daddy this was going to be it. My big break into showbizness...now look.'

He smiled, "Didn't you know you are up for the female version of Ironside."
I began to cry and couldn't stop, "Damn, I lost my one 'good' leg."

I cannot describe how I felt, it was almost like 'this could not be happening to me'. Wasn't I the one who was always on the go, making plans, making people feel good about themselves? And now – I laid in the bed and looked at my right leg-then I cried.

The longer I stayed in the hospital the longer I had one thing on my mind -I hated hospitals. What they need to do is make them cheery. You know, better color on the walls, better linens (Egyptian cotton would be nice), and get me a view!

Slowly the staff started getting me up, but I was lopsided – and I didn't want to look down and see that part. They kept saying, "You're looking better this morning." "Oh, looks like you got rest last night." "I see that your color has come back." Here I am, in a hospital bed without a wig, wearing no makeup or false eyelashes, and 'I look better this morning?' I would have looked better if I was in my own bed, smoking a cigarette, and had my leg still attached!

I fought anger, pity, resentment and death. Yes, that too. I wanted to live and die at the same time. I never told Tom this, but I so much wanted to scream, 'great, you all stand around two good legs and I lay here with one gone. Who is having a better day today?'

There were so many acts of kindness, though, like when I received a beautiful bouquet of yellow roses from Dennis (Organ Grinder). 'Keep grinding away, Gracie!'

I had my good days also – just not as many as the bad. And how can you, when you have a multitude of tubes stuck in you and you can't move easily. Oh, I tried to move my body, or should I say I tried to drag it. And when I needed to go to the bathroom, well, I graduated from a catheter to a bed pan. And the nurses were so encouraging, they'd say, "Look at you. You're making such progress." as they took away the bed pan. I so desperately to say, "Oh, thanks so much for wiping my ass."

After what seemed like forever, they let me go home. I first had to sit up on my own, eat a solid meal and keep it down, and be able to put on my dressing gown or robe by myself. Graduation day happened, Tom took off work, and between Sis and Tom we got home. I went straight to bed. I kept telling them both, "don't forget the pain killers – this is the only way we're <u>all</u> going to get through this!"

I started finding ways to sit up, move around, get in and out of the wheelchair and make it to the doctor's visits. It tired me out more than I have ever been tired, but I guess it's a good thing when you need to mend – you should sleep.

On one of the doctor visits we didn't go straight to my doc, we went to a center that was called Physical Therapy. I know, I haven't exercised in my life and <u>now</u> I have to. We got through the first session and when I got home I said, 'now I know why I never exercised before – it's work!'

Tom kept telling me how bad he felt that he couldn't help more. I kept telling him that someone had to bring in some money and keep the insurance active or else we'd be 'shit out of luck'. So, Sis took over. There were scheduled therapy sessions, three times a week. Once in awhile the doctor joined in to check on my 'progress.' He'd watch, then we'd go into a small room. He would fold his hands together and have a pleased look on his face, "Gracie, the therapist has kept me up on your progress and what I see is quite good, I think you are ready for the next step to recovery."
"Doc, this is not AA."
He said, "think of it as if it is."

"Okay, what is the next step of my recovery?"

"I want to send you to a clinic and have them make a prosthesis for you."

I hadn't even considered this – "you mean, replace the one that's been taken away?"

"Think of it as being able, eventually, to stand on your own two feet again."

"Okay, bring the dead leg on."

The 'fitting of the new leg' is worse than anything you can imagine. Some person takes a lot of measurements, asks you a lot of questions, and then you are asked to come back at another time. When you do come back, it's more measurements, more questions and then you are asked to come back again.

When you finally get the 'leg', it just lies there – it's dead.

As a child you learn to walk without thinking – you are told to stand and somehow you do, you are told to 'walk to me' and you do. Sometimes you fall, other times you don't but you almost do, so you grab on to something and make it.

The doctor had me get up on the examination table and he took off the bandages and measured my leg. I just closed my eyes. I tried with all my might to think of something that Totie Fields would say, "Say doc, isn't it nice to know a man finds my body still something to discover."

He looked at me and said, "Gracie, you're going to get through this, and I'm here to help you."

I pulled down my skirt and said, "I know what the alternative is, so just bring the god damn leg and let's see how we can make this work."

The next visit, the leg was waiting for me. Like I said, it was dead. It just laid on the table and I noticed that they didn't even try to match my skin tone.
To lighten things up, Doc said, "Gracie meet right leg, right leg, meet Gracie. This should be one hell of a fit." Then he looked at me and said, "ready?"
Instantly I said, "no."
He chuckled, "good."

With the help of the physical therapist the 'right leg met Gracie.' To try to describe the emotions in my body would or could not do justice to what was happening. Once the leg was in place, I was helped to stand – doc on one side, the therapist on the other. I was standing. That was a relief. With encouragement with such words as, 'now TRY and move.'
I tried.
I failed.
It didn't want to go with me.
But after several attempts, they got me to move a bit.
Exhaustion set in and I asked to be put in the wheelchair.
I covered my hands over my face. "I can't – I just can't."

The doctor, that kind man, pulled my hands from my face and said, "you will, you will."

I did try. It was probably the hardest thing I have ever had to do. That thing was part of you, so you had to make sure it worked with you, but most of the time it worked against you. "Now Gracie, try to remember to move your hip, kick the leg out, and that will get the new knee to bend."

"Good, now try to remember to give enough of a lift so that the tip of your shoe can clear the floor."

I failed.
"Almost, just remember, the knee has to lock in place so you can put weight on the new leg to move the other leg."

"I need a rest."

Session after session, it went on for months. Each time, I would go home to try it while no one was looking, only to start begging - no screaming - for help from Tom or Sis.

What I knew was that I was fat and that fat got in the way of recovery. But no matter how hard I tried, this leg that wasn't my leg, it was becoming my bad leg. Now I know they told me it would become part of me, and it would take time. But it wasn't becoming part of me. I tried, but I just couldn't do it. Kudos for those who can, I couldn't. I got frustrated, disappointed and really tired. All I wanted to do wa go back to bed.

So, after awhile, I said that I would rather take it slow. They both did a lot of encouraging, but soon, the new bad leg was gone. My real, good leg had been taken away from me, so, please, take this one away as well. Besides, I knew how to work the wheelchair and maneuver around with it.

Depression is an easy way out. But I wasn't going to allow that word to become part of me. Besides, hadn't Bette Midler done her stage show *Clams On The Half Shell* sitting in a wheelchair as a mermaid? People laughed and she got richer.

What about Totie Fields? When she battled her legs being gone, she moved on. She didn't let not standing on two feet bring her down. "I was built for sitting anyway."

So, I signed up for Comedy Workshops. One of the great things was that they were being held at the Pantages Theater on Hollywood Boulevard. An old vaudeville house turned into a movie theatre. I had hoped it would have been the Grauman's Chinese theatre, you know, where all the movie stars put their hand and feet prints, but I kept saying, "Honey, you may never make a movie that will screen here, but you can say that you did work here."

I'm glad there were only four or six sessions. After the surgeries my energy wasn't quite at its peak. But I needed to be there. The people of comedy were there and I needed to be part of this. There was Jay Leno, Betty Garret, Phil Foster [I gasped when I realized that I knew these people – they were on Laverne and Shirley, Laverne's dad and his girlfriend]. And you couldn't get better than who was producing it, the man who directed episodes of the Groucho Marx television show, 'You Bet Your Life, Robert Dwan.

And when I was there, in my wheel chair, no one treated me any different. We were there to 'work on comedy'. Some people think comedy is easy, but it's been said, comedy is the hardest form of entertainment, and I will tell you now, it is. A joke can be told many different ways, but if it's delivered right and you have the audience in your hand, not only is the audience laughing, but you are wanting to work harder at enjoying the time with them.

Sis, god bless her. She kind of ran away from Tom and me for awhile, but having her here made my life a bit easier, no, a lot easier. Not only did she put the wheelchair in and out of the car be part of our daily routines, I also asked her to take me down to the corner of Van Nuys and Victory Boulevard to pick up the Variety and Dramalogue magazines. After awhile, the guys there would have our newspapers ready as we drove up. They'd smile, be polite and make sure that I got 'the latest' gossip, stuff that wasn't printed in the papers.

Have you ever tried to maneuver in a wheelchair? You can't have stuff around. And after sitting in the wheelchair and not being able to just go somewhere, I started to realized that I truly was the worst housekeeper in the world. The kids would say it, in their own way, Tom would accept it, but now I know it.

The apartment was already small, but with the wheelchair it was impossible. We had to have a larger space. To give me something to do, it was agreed that I'd search the papers, make and set up the appointments. Then, Tom, Sis and I would go out and finding 'the right apartment'; and soon we did, a two bedroom one in Van Nuys. Here we go, moving again.

I didn't want to tell Tom or Sis, but I started noticing that I was having problems seeing. One evening I was watching the television and made a remark that caught Sis' attention. She handed me a newspaper and asked me if I would look up 'what was good on the television tonight.'

I looked down and, it was a blur. So I handed it back to her and said says, "Gracie, something's wrong isn't it?"

Well, off to the doc again. This time, an eye specialist. Not having a leg is one thing, not having eye sight is another. He came in after the exam and picked up the phone, "I am going to call your regular doctor while we are both here. He needs to agree on treatment."

I swallowed. Treatment?

What I gathered from the conversation is that I had hemorrhaging of the small blood vessels in the eyes known as diabetic retinopathy.

Immediately I thought, 'if things don't stop soon, diabetes is going to kill me.'

They both agreed that I should just do a couple sessions of a new treatment called laser surgery. 'You are awake during the whole procedure, we don't do any cutting and there should be little to no pain.'

My thought was, 'why couldn't they have done this with my leg?'

The one thing they tell you, 'your eyes will probably become sensitive to light, so bring sunglasses.'

I reached in my purse and told him, 'this is Hollywood, I have learned you never leave home without them.' The treatments seemed to help, and the eye doctor was right, it was almost painless.

After spending almost six months with us, Sis told us that she had to get back to her life. That life was in Portland, not LA. How could I blame her? She came down to help out, not to be an unpaid caretaker. I told her, "we'll manage – we would have had to with or without you." As she was leaving, my heart started hurting. Here was someone so unselfishly willing to sacrifice her life – mostly because of her worry for her father, I know, but I am hoping to be a bit of help for me, too. But we could always count on Sis, that's just the way Sis was – she cared about people. At that moment I wished she had been my daughter and that things in life would have been different.

While Tom worked, I managed. It wasn't easy, but others have done it, why couldn't Gracie. No, you didn't see the jewelry, wigs and fabulous dresses, what you saw was someone who was becoming a Plain Jane, and at that moment, that's all I could manage.

And then miracles of miracles, Bill decided to move down to LA and for awhile he stayed with us. Now, I don't know if it was to keep tabs on us or because he wasn't into the San Francisco scene, but he arrived on our doorstep announcing, "I'll be here just in case you need me." Bill, the middle child who was a Leo like me, was stubborn, independent, but also needed someone.

He came in the nick of time. I was worried for awhile how Tom and his heart were holding up. It's not that easy to care for an Italian, who is a diabetic, who has lost a leg and now has semi-bad eyes, and just what I expected, Tom suffered a mild heart attack. It scared the hell out of me. What would happen if Tom is gone and I'm left alone? This man had been my rock for almost twenty years. The doc assured us that it was very minor but "if at all possible avoid spicy food and stress."

I turned to Tom and said, "that means no more arguing about where we're going to eat Mexican food."

The doc agreed that was probably a good start.

During the holidays, Sis announced that she, in fact, will marry Don and that she would like us both at her wedding. It was hard to tell her that the day she chose was a doctor appointment day, "I live, breath and probably will die because of them." Without hesitation, she agreed to change her date. A plane trip seemed almost impossible, so, up the I-5 we went. It's not easy driving through the Siskiyou Pass by Ashland during that time of the year, but we made it.

Since I had made cakes for the kid's birthdays and special events, Sis asked if I would make her a wedding cake. I did a bit of the frosting and Tom did most of the rest – under my watchful eye. Not that he'd have eaten the cake, no, it's just that he wouldn't have made the cake as elegant as it should have looked.

Walter and Roc heard that we were in town and we went to their annual Christmas party. I think I shocked them a bit when we pulled up to their house and Tom had to go to the door. "Where's Gracie?"

"She's in the car."

"Well, tell her to get in here – what, she wants to make an entrance?"

"She will make an entrance, once she has some help."

Out came Walter and he found out that the reason I had to make an entrance was that there was no wheelchair ramp for me to get into the house. It's about 12 brick steps up and then another 6 wood steps. They have an incredible Victorian home, but they have not modified it for us cripples! I felt like queen for a day. They showed me some of the jewelry that they bought from the Kitty Geddes sale, the large dining room buffet that was now in their bedroom used for clothes, some stuff from the Hoyt auction, and I started to tear up. "They remember – they'll remember."

After we got back in the car I told Tom, "I want to come home."

"Portland is home to you now?"

"Well, yes and no. We have grandchildren who don't know us and I'd like to get to know them. And I miss my friends. There's nothing in LA for us anymore."

Tom said that couldn't happen for a couple years, as we needed him to keep working for insurance, for money and for his retirement. I didn't want to agree, but he was right. For the next two years, Bill would go and buy the Variety and Dramologue magazines. We'd sit around and gossip he helped me dream some dreams.

My health had stabilized, which was good thing. The wheelchair was my legs and Bill made me laugh more than I ever thought was possible. He seemed wicked and funny at the same time. One day he said, "Gracie, we're the same pea in the same pod – just different by who we love."

I wished I knew how to hug, or tell people that I loved them. I never really got that down. Oh, I tried in my own way: 'great job'; 'knew you could do it'; but right then I looked over and thought, 'these kids are really special – life dealt me a pretty good hand with them.'

He had mentioned a couple of times that house painting and looking after 'the parents' wasn't his idea of a 'lifestyle he wanted to live', and said he was moving back to San Francisco. Boy, I hated him to leave.

This was really the first time that I hugged Bill. I didn't want to say goodbye, I held him a bit longer and he said, 'watch it, it might rub off.'

'You're right – the next time I see you, you might be in feathers and boas.'

He whispered, 'how do you know that doesn't happen already?'

Now, I had never seen Bill wear a boa and to me he was as much of a man as I could have ever hoped for in a son.

Tom assured me that by May 1984 we'd move back home to Portland. I was more than ready. Sis came down to sort through our stuff and between Tom and Sis, we held a garage sale. You know, I said I'd never do another one – but after these years in LA, we had more stuff than we should have and out the door it was going to go.

During all of this, I called Sambo and he agreed to help us find a duplex and off moving we went again.

Tom Jr. and Sis' husband Don flew down to load the 26' Ryder truck; we rented a small trailer to pull behind the car. Tom Jr and Don took turns driving the truck, and Tom, Sis and I drove in the car.

I looked out the window toward the apartment and silently said goodbye. No more Hollywood dreams for Gracie. And I felt a tear drop from my eye.

I couldn't ride in the front seat, so I rode all the way to Portland in the back seat of the car – feeling like Sis was my chauffeur. "Feels like old times, going to the doctor, driving me home, drive me home, James."
She laughed, "you wish!"
I looked up and saw her looking back at me in the rearview mirror, "let's go home, Sis." And then I saw the smile that I had remembered from a little girl who didn't have a mom, and who probably wondered why I was now in her life. A little girl who was a pretty special woman now. "yeah, let's go home."
Tom just chuckled – his turn to drive was coming up in a couple hours and he knew it. Los Angeles to Portland is more than a day trip unless you don't have anything better to do.

We made it to Portland, or should I say Gresham, we didn't have a place to stay. Sambo had found us a storage unit for our stuff and also a motel room to rest our tired bodies. Don, the 'Toms' and Sis unloaded the truck, trailer and car into the storage unit. Later, we found a duplex in Wood Village. I was exhausted. I sat the whole way home and I was exhausted?

'When you make a decision,' my Mom used to say, 'you stick with it.' I had to abandon my dreams of Hollywood and now I was in this small duplex without any hope. The worse thing was that the ride up probably did more harm than good. I started getting very weak, always tired and soon it was hard for me to speak.

I was rushed to Gresham General Hospital. Going in and out of consciousness I think I heard the doctor saying that I had congestive heart failure and that possibly my lungs would fill with fluids and would have to be tapped. I was trying to find me during those days. Where was Gracie? Why hadn't she stood up and said,
"Hello, Suckers!" Why?

Within in a few days I felt alert, as if nothing had happened. Because the hospital wants your money but also wants you to stay as short a time as possible, they let me go home. Being in your own bed is the best cure for anything except getting better if you are already sick. My health became a yo-yo; good days and bad days. Sometime I wanted to sit up, eat and be me and other days I wanted to hibernate with the curtains closed and sleep.

I got up enough strength to go to Sambo's house for Thanksgiving. But once we got settled and the afternoon wore on into night I was exhausted again and had to get home. Christmas was not a holiday for me. I just wasn't with it, within an hour of getting over to Sambo's I needed to go back to bed.

As Tom pulled the comforter over me, I asked him to get hold of my doc in LA, I trusted him – certainly not the quacks in Portland. I felt like they were trying to kill me.

After arranging with the doc, and talking about how we were going to go through the Siskiyou Pass, Tom and I, once more, drove to Los Angeles.

This time it was his face looking back at me in the mirror, "can you hold on, mama?"

"I have so far, haven't I?"

What a trip – it was hard on both of us. Several long days on a road that no one likes to drive, through long stretches of nothing, and then you are greeted by the 'Grapevine', that steep climb to nothing to then find out you aren't in LA, but just outside it. We finally made it to LA on New Year's Day, and we went right to the hospital. Tom was so patient that even Job could take a lesson from him. Slowly, he got me out of the car and into the wheelchair. It was not easy, I know it, I was more of a wet noodle than a vibrant person, I was tired, sleepy and not good company. After getting checked in, I was taken right into a room, just like having one reserved just for me.

When the doc walked into the room, I felt a bit better -here was this kind man who had helped me in '79, so thank god he was here when I needed him in '85.

"Welcome back to these dreary rooms again."

"I see they still haven't livened up the place yet, now have they?"

"'fraid not – but with you here it will be a much cheerier place."

And lucky me, the room, nurses and food hadn't changed.

I was glad Tom had friends to stay with so I didn't have to worry about him. My head was actually too foggy to remember much.

But, I do remember right after I was put in a hospital gown, I was wheeled down and the tests began. It didn't take long before the doc sat Tom down next to my bed and said things I didn't want to hear, but were said just the same. "Grace, I'm sorry, but the left leg needs to be amputated, it has to be soon, as we can't wait any longer."

When doc left I looked over at Tom, "Daddy, I don't think I can go through another surgery, this is what happened to my Aunt Jo."

I felt my rock, lean over and whisper, "Mama, it will all be over when you have your surgery tomorrow. Just keep thinking positive thoughts." With that, I felt his lips on mine.

Per Carl Diana's personal notes: Page 1 ~~ Note dated 1-9-85
Sam Hansen
Grace died today
he call just a little bit ago
died today this afternoon. She was in the hospital. She is in California. Left last Sunday for California.
She was unhappy.
1:00 -- on the operating {table}
trying to save the other {leg}
her kidneys gave out
couldn't open a pill bottle
lungs filled up -- heart weaker & weaker
made a pact -- no seeing her -- no flowers --no funeral at -- Cremation etc.
She wants to be put on the desert.
real miserable --
Daddy -- "I going to die --" "can't stand the pain"

"You'd better be sure you really want something, because you might just wind up getting it."

Gracie, October 21, 1962

Famous Gracie quotes (or Gracie-'isms):

About her age: *"Just say I'm between eager and desire"* and later on in her years she would say, *"somewhere between eager and desperate!"*

At the sight of the World's Fair Expo in 1962:*"Diamonds are a girl's best friend -- but I'll never knock rubies, emeralds or pearls."*

About running against Tom McCall for Governor of Oregon, *"I've had my eye on [Governor] Tom McCall's seat for a long time."*

Slogan as she ran for Governor of Oregon, 1970: *"Gracie Hansen For Governor -- The Best Governor Money Can Buy."*

Her 'platform': *"Everyone in Oregon is entitled to and should have three things--something to work at, something to love and something to hope for."*

Her 'guilt complex': *"(I'm) working off a guilt complex. I feel guilty about all the things I didn't do for my parents when they were alive."*

About the world's Fair experience: *"Cinderella point in my life ... I came barreling in from Morton and my whole life changed. I've been enjoying it ever since"*

Her life achievement statement:*"I was fat and 40 and I came out of the hills and I made it. My message is this: if I could, who the hell can't?"*

In 1964, she almost ran for mayor of Seattle. Her slogan: *"I'm not going to open up the town, just your minds."*

In 1961 when trying to figure out how to raise funds to open her show, Gracie formulated what she called her 'pet theory' that: *"Science will never replace sex or cotton candy."*

About life: *"I believe people should raise a little more hell and a little less eyebrow."*

I wish to thank many people who have helped me with the play GRACIE as well as this book. I cannot express enough gratitude for the input, the searching and the gathering. Listed below are only a few of many.

Jeanette Gum, Gordon Malafouris, Maureen Cooper Slotto, George Barner, Jr., Walter Cole aka Darcelle XV, Roxy Leroy Neuhardt, Johnny Reitz, Portland Rose Festival, KGW Television (Rick Jacobs and Paul Kenney), KATU Television (Steve Denary), Multnomah County Library (Jennifer), Neeley's Antiques, Ron Wade, Candee's Nook (Caroline Moore), Mitzi Fairhart, Treasure Island Books (Dale and Tess Wentz), Harvey's Comedy Club (Marv), Dottie Fields, Bob Packwood, Vera Katz, Lenny Borer, Bud Clark, Will Vinton, Maggie White, Grethen Kaufory, Seattle Center Foundation (Todd Burley), Oregon Historical Society (Scott Daniels and Michele Kribs), Library of Congress (Megan Halsband), Lewis Co., WA GenWeb project (Jenny Tenlen), Washington State Archives (Benjamin Helle), KCPQTV13 (Keith Birdie), Center for Pacific Northwest Studies (Ruth Steele, Rozlind Kosther) , Seattle History (Carolyn Marr), Steve Miller (Hippo Hardware), Paula Gunness, David Rhianda, Phil Stanford, Will Vinton, Judy Keltner, Shari Shoman, and Bill Norvas, Jr. The Roaring 20's dancers: Carolyn Chordes Choate, Barbara [Bare] Smith, Goldie and of course Richard Hurst. Most of this book was written on the Island of Zakynthos, Greece, my second home.

I also thank all of you for allowing me the chance to share Gracie's story with you.

Please, in the future, archive! Or give it to your local archivist...it truly means a matter of detail or speculation.

The photos included in this book are from either Gracie's own collection or from Gordon Malafouris, Jeanette Gum or Maureen Slotto. Thank you from the bottom of my heart for keeping these.

Some background:

Carl Diana- Carl had an illustrious 52-year career as an attorney, beginning in 1953. He had many celebrated cases, including one in which F. Lee Bailey represented some of the parties, and another in which he represented Robert "Evel" Knievel. He was a co-founder of American Commercial Bank. Carl met and married Oliven Smith while in the Navy, in Memphis, Tennessee. They have 5 children, 6 grandchildren.

George Lester Barner, Sr. – Born, October 1890 (North Dakota) and died October 1974 in Olympia, WA. He was married twice, first marriage ended in 1930, with no children. Second marriage was with Mary Diana and lasted until her death in 1973; two children, Jeanette and George, Jr.

Jeanette Barner Gum - Born January 1938 (Centralia, WA). Married to Bob Gum 1934-2007; 7 children; 14 grandchildren and 5 great grandchildren.

George Barner, Jr. born August 1941 In Centralia, WA; lives in the family home in Olympia, WA.

Tom Cooper, Sr. Continued to have heart problems, had bypass surgery in 1986 and a fatal heart attack in 1991. Died at the hospital in Centralia, Washington, after visiting old friends in and around Morton, Washington.

Tom Cooper, Jr. Lives in Portland, Oregon; he has two daughters and three grandchildren.

Billy Cooper died from complications from AIDS in 1993.

Maureen Cooper currently resides in a small town in South Dakota.

Sam Hansen Born May 4, 1948; followed after his adopted Grandfather Sam Diana and owns his own barber shop. He is a father of two.

Leo Hansen Born April 15, 1913, died in Issaquah, Washington, January 31, 1974.

About the author

Donald I Horn aka Donnie is a playwright, author, director and producer (of well over 150 theatrical productions) and the founder of **triangle productions!,** a theatre company based in Portland, Oregon. His first book, *Crumbs of Love (and that's all you'll ever get),* was well received, and he is currently writing a sequel *Crumbs from the Table of Love.* He has written over fifteen plays and musicals, including *'69-The Sexual Revolution Musical* (which won two Portland Area Music Theatre Awards for Best Songs). He is a father of two boys (Jason and Nathan) and stepfather of three (Shawnee, Trisha and Sammy). He and his partner divide their time between homes in Portland, Oregon; Lincoln City, Oregon; Palm Springs, California, and Zakynthos, Greece. He holds a BA and MBA from City University, Seattle, Washington.

Proof

Made in the USA
Charleston, SC
19 September 2011